T0277600

Praise for
Unhappy Achiever

"A gentle reminder that one's dreams and needs can tell a person more about their worth and own definition of 'success' than external sources . . . relatable to [those] who are ready to loosen the girdle of traditions and expectations that keep so many women from living bigger, bolder lives. Readers will gravitate toward this book."

—Library Journal

"*Unhappy Achiever* is not just a book; it's a call to action for any woman who feels stuck in life and doesn't know where to turn. Ashley's journey mirrors our struggles and is a beacon of hope in our quest to return to our true selves. Her insights resonate deeply, making this soulful narrative a source of comfort and understanding. I encourage you to pick up a copy and allow her engaging storytelling to guide you on your own path of self-discovery."

—Nadine Macaluso, LMFT, PhD, author of
Run Like Hell: A Therapist's Guide to Recognizing, Escaping,
and Healing from Trauma Bonds

"*Unhappy Achiever* is a striking account of personal evolution, filled with hard-won insight. As Jordan explores love, loss, life, and liberation, readers will appreciate her raw honesty and her overarching message: Our value never lay in what we accomplished or who approved—and Pinterest-perfection pales next to the vibrant light of a woman who knows herself."

—**Dr. Kristi J. Smith,** author of *She Took a Turn: A Memoir of Climbing over Guardrails into Growth*

"Candid, raw, and deeply courageous, *Unhappy Achiever* unveils Ashley Jordan's journey from buried trauma to profound healing. Through her brave and intimate storytelling, she navigates the complexities of grief, loss, and the pursuit of inner peace, offering a guiding light for those seeking resilience and self-discovery after experiencing profound pain."

—**Jessica Zweig,** founder of SimplyBe. Agency and author of *Be: A No-Bullsh*t Guide to Increasing Your Self Worth and Net Worth by Simply Being Yourself*

"*Unhappy Achiever* is a courageous memoir that dismantles the illusion of external validation, revealing the profound truth that true happiness lies within our authentic selves. Ashley Jordan's journey is a powerful testament to the freedom that comes in shedding societal expectations and embracing inner fulfillment."

—**Keri Ohlrich, PhD, & Kelly Guenther**, authors of *Whatever the Hell You Want: An Escape Plan to Break Out of Life's Little Boxes and Live Free from Expectations*

Unhappy Achiever

Unhappy Achiever

Rejecting
the Good Girl Image
~~and~~

*and Reclaiming the Joy
of Inner Fulfillment*

Ashley Jordan

WONDERWELL

Copyright © 2024 by Ashley Jordan

24 25 26 27 28 5 4 3 2 1

All rights reserved. No part of this book may be reproduced, stored in a
retrieval system or transmitted, in any form or by any means, without the prior
written consent of the publisher.

Library of Congress Control Number: 2023910523

ISBN 978-1-63756-043-3 (hardcover)
ISBN 978-1-63756-044-0 (EPUB)

Editor: Olivia Bartz
Cover and interior design: Adrian Morgan
Cover image: Shutterstock
Author photograph: Jessica Kaminski, The Refinery Photo Studio

Published by Wonderwell in Los Angeles, CA
www.wonderwell.press

WONDERWELL

Printed and bound in Canada

To Daniel John,

whose memory and unconditional love are eternally etched in me.

To Ari, Alexandra, and Ashton,

the beautiful, living, breathing embodiments of my heart in the world.

To Aaron,

for reading every chapter of this book as it was written, and for loving me so well in marriage and divorce.

To Ashley

(Berman) Kinney—my former self—for being who you needed to be to survive until your authentic self was strong enough to step forward.

To my soul sisters,

who saved me when I wasn't sure I could save myself.
You are the sacred feminine. You are divine.

Finally, this book is for all the *fearless women*
who dare to be free.

Contents

Achievers Anonymous

You're not one success, milestone, or promotion away from happiness.
What you've spent a lifetime striving for has been yours all along.
That feeling you're chasing—that evasive goal, whatever it is for you—
it already resides in you. You are "it." And you always have been.

A m I an unhappy achiever?

Asking myself this question changed the course of my life.

Less than two years into my career as a writer, the *New York Times*—the holy grail of bylines—published one of my pieces. This came after late nights spent writing while the kids slept, countless literary workshops, and submitting to press after press for the past few years all because of a promise I made to myself: if my work and literary talent could be validated by one of the most prestigious news media outlets in the world, this time I would have "made it." In reality, when I saw my name published next to the most personal prose I'd ever written, I didn't feel the way I thought I would.

It was the *New York Times* . . . but I felt no excitement. No surge of confidence. No sense of satisfaction. Instead, I felt the same.

Worse, I felt empty.

What's wrong with me? I wondered. *I've reached a milestone most writers dream of, and I did it in record time, so why am I not more thrilled? Energized? Fulfilled?*

I couldn't understand what was happening. In a moment of panic and desperation, I turned to a universally hallowed source of information for an answer:

Google.

Without judgment or reservation, Google had always provided me with answers to my life's most burning questions. *Did Meghan and Harry make Oprah Lilibet's godmother? What are the best ways to remove dry foot skin?* And this time, *What is it called when you experience a significant achievement and feel nothing?*

A brutally honest answer appeared in the form of an article titled "Are You an Unhappy Achiever?" As I read, I began to feel an uncomfortable awareness. A reckoning occurred between the deeply ingrained beliefs I held around my own success and my heart's response to the question I'd been asking myself for months: *Have I ever been genuinely happy?* By the end of the article, there was no backpedaling or denying the truth—I was an unhappy achiever.

And I wasn't alone either. As I thought about my family, friends, and colleagues, it became clear that we all hungered for the same sorts of things. The menus we made for ourselves might have varied from person to person, but the voracious appetites we sought to satisfy with achievements didn't. We were all searching for something to make the nagging hunger pangs—the persistent inner restlessness—stop.

Below this article were dozens upon dozens of pieces on the topic, with words and phrases like "success hangover," "unsatisfied," and "high anxiety" leaping out at me. From what I could gather, the Internet defined unhappy achievers as people who are addicted to the accolades, validation, and approval that accompany achievement but ultimately feel exhausted and deeply unfulfilled.

Over the next few days, I began to see how almost every decision in my life had been guided by an unrelenting quest for personal and professional success. I had spent thirty-seven years driven by a perpetual lust for the perfect blend of accolades to feed an internal engine that mostly ran on empty. And once I saw it, I couldn't unsee it.

Striving had always been part of some unspoken effort to "arrive." I worked toward my goals, focusing on the belief that reaching them might make me happy, impressive, and most of all, complete. I told myself that if I worked a little harder—if I reached another milestone—I would finally feel like I was enough.

I was unhappily achieving in my early elementary school years with an age-inappropriate panic over getting into a good college. In junior high and high school, I fixated on becoming a basketball star. In college, I turned my attention toward getting into law school. After earning a full scholarship to law school, my focus shifted to passing the bar exam and becoming a licensed attorney. Then, my obsession moved on to marriage and motherhood; both of these became new boxes to mark off on the continually growing checklist of my life.

Along the way, I earned all kinds of accolades, big and small. Captain of my high school basketball team. Hometown beauty queen. Northern Illinois University Outstanding Woman Student. Best oral argument performance in my law school's trial competition. I worked hard to achieve in ways I thought would make me worthy of others' approval. But no matter how many gold ribbons I won, I didn't think I was valuable or lovable.

Achievements can be another means to avoid the harshest realities of our lives. In this sense, they're not so different from more illicit measures people take in their quest to avoid difficult emotions. The more I used achievements as a buffer between myself and past pain, the more the world around me rewarded me with attention. The accolades and approval made me feel special and significant for a second. But as with any drug, over time, the highs became shorter and harder to come by, and the lows became deeper and more difficult to dig out of. An externally focused life was a hollow life. Instead of finding the love and worthiness I desired, I discovered an abiding sense of emptiness, absence, and anxiety.

The more I reflected on my own preoccupation with achievement, the more I realized we are conditioned to believe that who we are isn't as important as what we do, so we seek love and acceptance through doing. Yet no matter how much we accomplish, we feel dissatisfied, wondering what's missing and what we're doing wrong.

We're taught to believe happiness is ours for the taking *if*. If we go to college and become a degreed professional. If we marry someone respectable and decent. If we become the proud parents of two children. If we buy a nice house in a picturesque neighborhood. If we land our dream job, get promoted, or make partner. We spend decades, even lifetimes, believing: *If I can just do—or have—or become—that one thing, I'll be satisfied, content, complete.*

For women, added pressure to be "good," "nice" girls substantiates this myth. Good girls are pleasing. Good girls seek praise. Good girls are shiny. Good girls make their parents proud. Good girls assume an inauthentic image when who they are, what they think, or what they want isn't seen as good or nice enough by others. We're brought up believing that good girls get rewarded with fairy-tale lives, and that the antidote to unhappiness is simply more goodness.

She who is everything to everyone and nothing to herself.

She who puts her family first and herself last.

She who accepts people's leftovers as love.

She is a good girl.

In the end, we find ourselves trapped on an invisible hamster wheel of achievement. We're spinning all the time and can't see that we're going nowhere. We bounce from goal to goal, objective to objective. Yet every mission accomplished feels more anticlimactic than the last. We are the people "doing" ourselves to death, sacrificing health and relationships to arrive at some ultimate (albeit elusive) point of existence. No matter how much or what we do, genuine satisfaction evades us. And the parts of us we sought to fill with wealth, power, goodness, and praise somehow feel emptier than before.

I spent most of my life ingesting the myth bought and sold by capitalist culture that what was missing inside me could be fixed by something outside me. Then, shortly after my thirty-seventh birthday, I cracked open. An unexpected trigger sent me spiraling into the traumatic grief I had buried when I was thirteen years old. Suddenly, a shattering emotional hurt I had stowed away in the depths of my core came bleeding out, and the decades that separated me from a devastating death I had never mourned vanished, and it was as if it had all happened yesterday. When my past became present, I was reminded of a love that was innocent, unconditional, and timeless. And I came to realize that love, in its purest forms, isn't earned by what we do, have, or become. It's ours by virtue of our being. The light we feel on our faces in the presence of unspeakable joy doesn't beam down on us from a source separate from ourselves; it's our own light reflecting back on us.

Everything I needed to be, I *was* already—at thirteen, at thirty-seven. I was everything I needed to be the moment my soul made its home in my body.

Unhappy Achiever is an intimate story about my spiritual reckoning in the wake of this realization. It is the story of how a unique (yet universal) blend of old wounds and social conditioning caused me to construct a version of myself that was different from who I was meant to be. It is the story of how the protective masks we wear keep us disconnected from ourselves and those around us; and how it's only when we live into the truth of who we are that we can discover the magic, wisdom, and wholeness of our lives.

Unhappy Achiever is the story of my crucible. It is about how I learned to stop *doing* and discovered the beauty of *being*. When we make that change, we discover that the freedom our souls seek only resides in radical authenticity. And that struggle and suffering can be powerful catalysts for reclaiming who we were born to be before the world forced us to forget. It is liberation and initiation. It is a baptism unto ourselves.

The chapters that follow depict my journey from an unhappy achiever to a woman rebuilding a life that lights her up from the inside out (instead of the outside in); getting out of her head and back into her heart; and becoming a happier, more healed human. In the personal experiences and anecdotes on these pages, I share my inner and outer transformation, an evolution that unfolded in ordinary and extraordinary ways in my everyday life.

My intention is to use storytelling to compel you to forge your own richer, more authentic, and soulful lives. When we see ourselves in other people's stories, we're reminded that we're not alone. Although the facts and circumstances of our lives may differ, no human experience is truly unique. Storytelling takes universal threads of lived experiences and weaves them into tapestries of learning and inspiration. I hope you will see that if one woman can conjure up the courage to upend every aspect of her existence—from her friendships to her career to her marriage— to make her life truer and more reflective of her deepest desires, then you can make courageous changes (big or small), too.

May these stories inspire you to reject the suffocating box of "good" and reclaim the love, joy, and fulfillment inherent in your own breath-taking *being*.

—Ashley

Part One:

—

Being
Good

CHAPTER 1

Wombs & Wounds

——————

I didn't know the price of all that achieving was authenticity. Even if I had, I was too desperate for my mother's approval to care.

My mother told me she loved me—I just wasn't sure she liked me. It was a painful, persistent suspicion, one that was a staple of my adolescence. Neither of us ever acknowledged it, but it loomed between us like an invisible barrier to the full breadth of our bond.

I'm not sure nurturing was something my mother knew how to do, so I don't fault her for a childhood lacking in maternal nourishment. But the result was that I became a young woman deprived of a love she desperately desired.

I imagine I experienced the same malaise my mother must have suffered from after being raised by a woman whose own mother died suddenly when she was nine years old. This was a painful, yet palpable, part of our family's past that was rarely discussed, least of all by my grandmother. That's often the way it goes with wounds that wall off our hearts. They impact us profoundly, and silently, affecting the rest of our lives in insidious ways. My great-grandmother's unexpected death at forty years old led to at least a few generations of women who craved a mother's love that their ancestor's fate cost them. Every woman is another woman's child, after all.

Although I understand my mother might not have been able to give me a gift she never received, this absence of affection was hard. Early in my childhood, my parents' roles became clear. My mother was in charge: She managed the money, issued the final pronouncement on major decisions, and made sure our material needs were met. She was also my principal disciplinarian, a duty she either didn't or couldn't delegate to my dad. If my mother was the lead actor in our family saga, my father was a supporting castmate. He was a participatory parent and partner, but his role was ancillary.

I respected my mother for doing the dirty work of discipline, and I didn't think much about it. But years later, my therapist said something that made me pause.

I had recounted a memory from when I was four or five years old. I'm unclear on my crime or the specifics of my mother's response. But I know her reprisal was harsh enough to send me running from our first-floor bathroom shortly after getting out of the shower. I sought refuge in the basement with my father. Still dripping wet, I nestled into the safety of his familiar embrace.

"Aw, what's wrong, Puddin'?" he asked, holding me so tight it seemed safe to let tears stream down my baby-faced cheeks.

"Jack!" my mother shouted from upstairs. "Don't enable her bad behavior!"

My dad didn't loosen his embrace. It was an instance in which my father disregarded my mother's demands in favor of doting on his daughter. He rescued me at that moment. And I felt like I'd been an escapee seeking sanctuary, running from an enemy or oppressive order I didn't understand—a maternal regime based on my purported best interest, but sometimes so strict it broke my sensitive spirit.

"My mother was hard on me, but she had to be," I said, following a short recitation of the shower incident.

"Really? Why did she have to be?" my therapist asked.

"Well, my dad didn't do much in the way of discipline. So, my mom had to do the hard work of it."

"Hard?" My therapist sounded puzzled. "Did she have to be so strict with you? Were you particularly hard to manage as a preschooler?"

I didn't know how to respond. The answer was, "No, I wasn't an unusually difficult preschooler." I was shy and tender. I don't think I was any harder to handle than any other young child, even if something about me might have made me more difficult for my mother to love. I was innocent and seeking solace from a part of my upbringing that already seemed rigid and restrictive. At this young age, I began to understand that the appearance of perfect behavior was more important than how I felt.

Appearances, I would learn, were synonymous in my mother's mind with affection. My mother told me once about a pair of *groovy* shoes she'd desperately wanted as a young girl. My grandmother said no to the fad footwear at first because she found them ugly. Still, my mother insisted she needed them to fit in at a new junior high school. My grandmother reluctantly acquiesced, and my mother was thrilled—until she discovered that the fashion trend hadn't made its way to the rural farming community her family moved to. No one at her new school had the coveted shoes, and suddenly, what had seemed groovy wasn't actually so groovy, after all.

When my mother told me this story, she highlighted the irony of believing the new shoes would make her popular in a new school. But the deeper meaning lay in receiving the shoes from my grandmother. Being given something that meant so much to her but that seemed senseless and silly to my grandmother had made my mother feel loved. In this way, the material turned into something sacred for my mother.

And so my mother showed love through material things, too.

She worked hard to buy me beautiful clothes, and the unspoken bargain for such benevolence was obedience and being "good." I lived in a nice, clean home. I was well fed and outfitted to perfection, so, in her view, there was no cause for complaint. Whenever I acted out in response to a craving for maternal tenderness, the penalty for bad behavior was being labeled a brat.

I didn't want to be a brat. I didn't want to be ungrateful. I didn't want to be bad. I wanted to be good—good enough that maybe, one day, the material gifting would start to flow over into unconditional love. I recall riding in the back seat of my parents' car at six years old, thinking: *I can't wait until I'm sixteen. When I'm sixteen, I can have a boyfriend.* Although I couldn't necessarily identify it as a child, I see now that I wasn't longing for a boyfriend in kindergarten. I was longing for someone to love me. To see me. To wrap me in warmth and tenderness. To tell me I was beautiful without being perfect.

Appearing perfect was important to my mother, and having an overweight kid didn't fit with this vision. She took me to Lynn's Fit 'n Trim, a weekly weight-loss support group where the extra pounds on my prepubescent body melted away in a matter of months.

"Sliver leads to slice, slice leads to slab, slab leads to slob," Lynn would tell us.

Lynn's group, and the low-fat diet my mother meted out to me, magically undid the effects of all the sedentary years I'd spent sitting on babysitters' couches snacking on Cheetos. Losing weight meant being noticed instead of being ignored. It was as if people had looked past me because they couldn't be bothered to pay attention to someone whose physical form was unappealing to them. Shortly after my socially sanctioned and maternally motivated weight loss, my mother and I went shopping for a new wardrobe, and I traded in baggy silk blouses and stretch pants for bodysuits and skinny jeans. Almost overnight, people applauded my appearance.

But the problem of being too big for my family still plagued me. My grandmother never missed an opportunity to remark: "Gosh, Ashley, you'd never know you used to be fat." I may have been skinny on the outside, but on the inside, I still felt the same seething insecurity of my formerly "fat" self.

Maybe I couldn't erase the past, but I reveled in the attention my new physique afforded me. Instead of numbing my sense of inadequacy with food, I craved additional admiration because it all began to look a lot like love. And I believed I'd become someone everyone found more lovable, or at least noticeable.

Perhaps, that's part of what led to a lifelong passion for pleasing. If love wasn't free, I figured I could get really fucking good at earning it. If my being too big made me unworthy, then I'd prove my worthiness by staying small—and doing big things. In that way, I set out to show the world (and myself) that I wouldn't suffer from a shortage of love and affection any longer. If love was synonymous with adulation and success, I'd strive to be brilliant. I'd strive to be pretty. I'd strive to be skinny. I'd strive to be accomplished. And I'd strive to be someone my mother might like—and love—a lot more.

I didn't know the price of all that achieving was authenticity. Even if I had, I was too desperate for my mother's approval to care.

When we realize our mothers are the source of our wounds, we struggle. We writhe in discomfort between our lived reality and all the portrayals of perfect mothers. The broken promise of a model mother pisses us off because we're socialized to believe such a mother was our birthright. And that being biologically bestowed upon a woman who wasn't a modern marvel of a mother—but a mere mortal—cheated us out of something that might have made us happier, healthier, and more whole.

But our happiness, health, and wholeness belong to us. They're not contingent upon our mothers' love, or lack thereof. The lesions many mothers unwittingly leave behind later become the lessons that lead us home to ourselves.

My mother is one of my greatest teachers. Not receiving the unconditional love, nurturing, and nourishment I longed for from her is forcing me to learn to love, nurture, and nourish myself more deeply. I should no more lament my parents for not being everything I wished them to be than waste time lamenting that I won't be everything *my* babies wish me to be. I can't promise my three children a perfect mother, any more than my mother could pledge the same to me. Because I am no more a perfect mother than I am a perfect person.

The ideal of perfect parents is an illusion.

It's only when we step out of that illusion that we can assess our own wounds. Acknowledging and accepting the imperfections of our mothers allows us to mother the most precious parts of ourselves in ways that the women who raised us never could. Eventually, the pain they inflicted subsides and creates space for our own inner sanctuaries. And we begin to understand that their love, approval, or lack thereof has nothing to do with our worth—and everything to do with their wounds.

CHAPTER 2

Barbies & Bastards

Being a nice Midwestern girl meant being someone else most of the time. So I created a version of me that was unequivocally other than my true self, a representative to perform social interactions on my behalf. I called her Amber.

"You bastard!" I swung Barbie's stiff, cupped palm until it smacked against Ken's tanned cheek.

"Ashley!" my mother gasped. She dropped the laundry she was folding to peer down at me. "That's not a nice word."

"Sorry," I said. Embarrassed, I lowered my head, hoping if I avoided her stare long enough, I'd melt away into the floor amid the sea of blond, frizzy-haired Mattel dolls, and she'd forget about my shameful infraction.

I didn't know what a bastard was. My only reference point was the soap operas my chain-smoking babysitter watched where heroines shout it at scorned lovers. On serials like *General Hospital*, *All My Children*, and *One Life to Live*, *bastard* was uttered with impunity and as frequently as words like *baby* and *beautiful*.

Although it hadn't been clearly defined for me, I knew it was something angry women said to men who wronged them. And in the context of my dolls' storyline, Ken had made Barbie angry, so, logically, he was a bastard.

Still, I'm not sure what was more humiliating. That I was ignorant about the word's meaning, or that my mother said my language was

15

something other than nice.

Growing up in a Midwestern family, I knew the word *nice* was supposed to describe me. *Nice* was synonymous with *good*. *Good* was synonymous with *girl*, and "good girls" were also "nice girls." I was a good girl, or at least, I tried very hard to be. And as I'd just learned, good girls dare not speak the word *bastard* aloud. I dutifully eliminated it from my elementary vocabulary.

But what if Ken really was behaving like a bastard? And what if Barbie wanted to tell him so? Was there no possibility in my mother's mind that Barbie's use of the word, and resulting rage, could've been justified? I wouldn't ever find out. I silenced Barbie, like I silenced myself.

Being a nice Midwestern girl meant being someone else most of the time. So, I created a version of me that was unequivocally other than my true self, a representative to perform social interactions on my behalf. I called her Amber.

Amber was polite and accommodating. She wasn't the girl chastised for being bossy in kindergarten when she stepped up to lead her friends during free play. Amber was serious most of the time, except in instances where she felt comfortable enough to let her dry sense of humor and silliness sneak out.

Most of all, though, Amber was quiet and deferential. She listened and submitted to the voices of everyone else, never stopping to question whether those voices were acting in her best interest or theirs.

The first time being Amber seemed safer than being Ashley was after a day I spent playing at the home of my aunt who often babysat me. When it was time to clean up, she told me her son, who was a few years younger than I was, wasn't responsible for the mess he and I made together, and I'd need to clean it up by myself. She left the room and closed the door, and I picked up the toys, one by one. As I worked, I talked to myself.

I recited a string of hurts I harbored against her, not just from that day, but from days past. All the times she had made me a punching bag to beat out her bitterness and burning family resentments. The times she told me I was too much or too spoiled. The humiliating mealtimes in which she criticized me for overeating. Pain poured out of my young psyche like a song. And for a moment, I was lost in a rhythm of unrepressed emotions.

Suddenly, the bedroom door burst open, reminding me where I was. My aunt looked down at me on the floor, still sifting through the mess, and glared.

"I heard everything you said," she said. It was as if there had been a trial and she had found me guilty. "I could hear you through the heating vent."

"I . . . I'm sorry . . . I didn't mean it!" I said. "I was just mad!"

The glaring intensified. "We say what we really mean when we're angry, Ashley."

Then she left me alone again with the mess.

That's when I decided it was best not to say how I felt, that revealing what I thought could be dangerous. Even if I'd intended to be heard, my aunt's reaction made it clear I wouldn't be listened to, and now I had to clean up two messes instead of one: a pile of toys and repercussions from my childish attack on an adult's ego. So, I sacrificed my voice, instead of speaking my truth. And I made sure Amber always said what everyone else wanted to hear, even when it contradicted her reality and ran counter to what she felt in her heart. Amber searched for truth externally, believing it could only be found in other people's judgments and opinions.

The more I used my Amber persona to deal with the world around me, the more Ashley disappeared. The more I evaporated, the more I convinced myself that Amber was the real me. The line between Amber and Ashley became so thin and faint I could barely discern where she ended and I began. Like the titular character in Greta Gerwig's *Barbie* movie, I believed that my authenticity belonged in a box. Amber was that box. Amber was the Barbie version of me—a perfect, plastic automaton who replaced Ashley.

I was still contemplating whether Barbie's outburst against Ken was warranted when my mother interrupted my playing again.

"Ashley, we need to talk about something. Your teacher wrote a note." Faster than Doc Holliday could pull a pistol in a gunfight, she produced a stack of stapled papers. On top was a math test so covered in red ink it looked like evidence in a murder investigation. "Do you recognize this?" she asked, already sounding like a prosecutor about to make her case.

"Ummm . . . I think so," I said.

"Well, look," she said, gesturing to the top of the first page, next to a red *C* that appeared to have been written much larger than necessary. I leaned in to make out the words my teacher had scrawled: *Ashley, your grades are slipping!*

"She says your grades are slipping," my mother recited, as if I couldn't read it just fine myself.

"Okay," I said, not knowing what else to offer.

What was she hoping to hear? I actually hadn't seen the test before, and my shame made me speechless. My grades were mostly good, so this test and its ominous warning about my academic decline were distressing. I had always tried my best to please. Pleasing was all I—or, more accurately, Amber—did. And being pleasing required earning exemplary grades. Succeeding in school or anywhere else meant approval and attention. Approval told me who I was and what I was, so I didn't have to wonder and worry. If I couldn't find myself anymore, approval let me know I still existed. I was a smart girl, because I earned praise. I could collect my achievements one by one and stow them away until their accumulation convinced me I was someone people loved. Maybe I could even love myself.

But at that moment I could only stare blankly at the note from my teacher until tears pooled in my eyes. The math problems I'd missed were so glaring, they jumped off the page and taunted me, as if saying: *The gig is up. You're not so smart, after all.*

My fragile sense of self was under assault. I stared at the proof of intellectual inferiority for a few more seconds before I couldn't take it any longer. I burst into tears. "Now, I'll never get into a good college!" I cried.

I was in the third grade.

I was already crumbling under the weight of adult aspirations before I'd even begun puberty. I didn't know much about college, but I was very aware that attending was a nonnegotiable family expectation. Those sorts of externally imposed presumptions felt like constraints on my future and left little room to build a home inside of me. Instead, space that should have been filled by my own fantastical youthful dreams, designs, and whims was cluttered by pressure, perfectionism, and other people's plans.

I didn't need to worry about college in the third grade. I needed to know I had support to develop a strong sense of self. Now, when I think about nine-year-old me, I reassure her that we are more than arbitrary measures such as academic standards. That our intelligence and talents are too vast to be graded. That our own unique, exquisite realness transcends the artificiality of any Barbie. And our worth is too great to be tied to the love and approval of bastards.

CHAPTER 3

Pastors & Priests

———

Pastors, priests, and parochial school sometimes left me feeling
like maybe God didn't see me. Like I was someone to be conditionally
judged, rather than unconditionally loved. Like my gender was
biblically cursed, instead of divinely inspired.

After being ushered back to a dimly lit confessional room, all I could make out was the silhouette of a priest. My eight-year-old self was petrified. Suddenly, memories of my most recent sins escaped me as the pressure to provide some solid source of shame mounted.

"Bless me, Father, for I have sinned. This is my first confession," I recited. Then I devolved into an awkward stutter.

"I . . . I . . . I lied to my parents," I lied.

The words fumbled out of my mouth as if the Holy Spirit was trying to stop the utterance and save me from turning my penitence into an original sin. Unfortunately, Divine intervention was no match for sheer will. I decided I'd rather lie to a priest about a lie I hadn't told than look foolish because I couldn't think of a single sin to repent for. The fact that my eagerness to please compelled me to lie in my first (and only) Catholic confession mortified me. I worried that carrying out such a heinous crime in the presence of God would count against my newly tortured soul tenfold.

To say Catholicism made me anxious and uncomfortable as a kid would be an understatement: it scared the hell out of me.

My first communion had been similarly traumatic. As I'd prepared to receive the consecrated body and blood of Christ in the form of stale bread and grape juice, my anxiety had spiraled with each step closer to a stern woman with a hairdo probably popular in the late 1800s, who was assisting the priest in administering the Eucharist. Still, I continued my reluctant approach until I stood in front of her. Unsure what to do, I reached out for her bowl of bread chunks, but she swatted at me in disgust. She turned my palm upward and placed broken bread in my quivering, cupped hand, her steely eyes drilling into me.

After that, I lost my appetite for the Lord's Supper.

Lucky for me, my parents left the Catholic Church (for the Lutheran Church) when I was in junior high school. Our family's church attendance was sporadic at best, so my encounters with priests were limited. However, attending a Lutheran elementary school made my run-ins with pastors far more frequent.

My school pastor was quiet and kind. But he was also conflict avoidant, or at least that's what his reluctance to condemn the bad behavior of his congregants suggested. He certainly had no idea what to make of an adolescent girl asking him why women weren't allowed to become pastors in the Lutheran church. When I asked the question out of genuine curiosity, he was speechless.

Maybe he just didn't have the stomach to look a young female student in the eyes and tell her that God doesn't deem her fit to be a church leader based on her sex. Regardless, I took his lack of response to mean that either my questions weren't worth answering, or *I* wasn't worthy.

Despite being disillusioned with men of the cloth, God stirred inside me growing up. This God wasn't the foreboding figure patriarchy imposed upon me. This God was a woman, an all-loving Mother. I confided in Her every night before bed, and every now and then, She whispered back. I chose to believe She heard me, even if some men leading congregations in Her name didn't care to. Talking to Her provided some welcome respite from the muzzling confinement of church and school.

The compulsory silencing that often accompanies religious dogma wasn't insidious at my elementary school; it was apparent, made manifest anytime teachers stuck masking tape on the mouths of students who spoke out of turn. From our voices to our clothes, anything resembling free self-expression was at best constrained, and at worst, forbidden.

Priests, pastors, and parochial school sometimes left me feeling like God didn't see me. Like I was someone to be conditionally judged rather than unconditionally loved. Like my gender was biblically cursed instead of divinely inspired. Like my voice was meant to be measured and restrained, not liberated and true. Like my soul could somehow be destined for damnation, when I knew it was already guaranteed a place in heaven.

Spirituality in its healthiest forms—whether connecting with nature, lighting candles in a local church, or meditating in a monastery—is as central to our existence as breathing. When we abandon our spirituality, something in us tends to suffer. I'm not advocating for any sect, denomination, or doctrine. I'm certainly not encouraging anything hateful or fear mongering. I'm merely suggesting that spirituality allows us to see our place within a bigger, more beautiful plan or purpose.

We are moral wisdom keepers; arbiters of ancient psalms, mysticism, and magic. A "good" book of someone else's life isn't the only way to testify to our souls' self-evident truths. Communing with our own holiness can be as precious as any other devotional practice. It doesn't matter whether we choose to attend a house of worship one day a week or seek solace in inner silence, as long as our spiritual expression is empowering and authentic. That sanctified site inside us where our Spirit lives belongs to everyone and no one, so mine is a space now solely reserved for the goddess in me.

And more and more, I'm realizing She was my redemption all along.

CHAPTER 4

Best Friends, Burials & Beloveds

The sacred lessons Dan and his death taught me had nothing to do with external sources—and everything to do with learning how to source myself. I became my own best friend and my own light in the darkness—and, most of all, my own beloved.

Somehow, all the heartache in our lives doesn't seem so hard to bear when we're blessed with one beloved best friend.

Dan was that person for me from the moment we met in first grade. He was a best friend and beloved, bundled into one brilliant, smiling, stunning spirit. My reflection sparkled in his eyes as if I was made of crystals instead of cells. While others told me my body was too big, so I shouldn't try to burn so brightly, Dan's love provided the single source of evidence that beauty resided in me.

Not having developed the inner authority necessary to attest to that myself, I soaked up every second of time spent with someone who made me smile and both saw and brought out my sparkle more than anyone else ever had. Our bond warmed me from the outside in. I channeled its electric current as long as I could, drawing comfort from the fact that even if no one else ever noticed the light in me, Dan did. *I am worthy of love*, I reasoned. *The way Dan looks at me, our junior-high dates, his letters—they all told me so.*

Then one day, without warning, the light went out.

Dan was riding on his ATV on the private airfield near his home, when a landing plane struck and killed him.

On my thirteenth birthday, I stood over Dan's coffin, barely seeing him through my half-closed eyes. It hurt too badly to see the reality of his young, lifeless body in front of me. Shock and disbelief competed with the fear of what it would be like to move forward without the truest friend and love I'd known. The feeling in my gut was agony, and I wondered whether I was going to pass out or throw up.

Dan had been dressed in a pale-blue collared shirt, and someone had tucked a baseball, a symbol of the sport he loved most, by his side.

"He looks so peaceful, like he's sleeping," I heard someone behind me whisper. Everything in me wanted to rage and scream: "He doesn't look like he's sleeping, you idiot! He looks like he's dead!"

His face, painted with makeup, looked paler than normal; the ivory foundation the mortuary cosmetologist applied couldn't reproduce the olive undertones of his complexion. His lips were too red with lipstick, and I wondered if it was better to see him one last time like this or whether the trauma of witnessing this caricature was worse than never seeing his sweet face again.

I don't know how long I stood over him. I was cemented in place until one of my parents turned to step away. As soon as they signaled it was time to leave, I was struck by simultaneous waves of relief and panic. I was desperate to escape the death before me, but I didn't want to separate from him. And I didn't want him to leave me behind. Every fiber of my being wanted to leap into his casket, slam the lid shut, and be buried alongside him.

Dan's death was a wrench in my soul. The love between us was deeper and more mature than our years. The words we wrote to each other, the costume-jewelry ring he took from his grandmother's collection that sat on my small finger, the sound of his voice during endless hours on the phone—it all felt like home. It was a safe space I craved and counted on as a young girl who spent most of her childhood struggling to be seen.

Dan was anything but unseen. He was smart, funny, and charismatic. People gravitated toward him and his penchant for making mischief. He could accept love in a way I couldn't. I didn't know what it felt like to be noticed like that. For most of my childhood, he was the only one who seemed to notice me at all. I could barely believe that of all the people he might have loved, he chose me.

But as we grew up and found ourselves on the verge of becoming teenagers, the intensity of our love scared me. I didn't understand how two kids could devote themselves to each other so completely and unconditionally, so young. I worried about where it would lead and whether it was even real. Maybe if I'd known that Shakespeare's Juliet was only twelve years old when she met Romeo, or that Dolly Parton met her husband at eighteen, I would have found it easier to trust a love I'd known since I was seven. Dan appeared to understand it better than I did. He seemed completely confident in the unbreakable bond between us, as if the flame burning in our innocent hearts could never burn out. But I worried that it would engulf us both.

So, rather than risk getting burned, I withdrew. A few weeks before Dan's death, I'd started pushing him away. I canceled our dates and ignored his phone calls. I made him go away—and then he was truly gone.

I never had the chance to say goodbye, or to tell him I loved him and how much he meant to me. I never told him his love had been steadily healing my gaping internal wound with its slow, steady bleed. The guilt and regret I felt after his death led me to wonder if losing him completely was the painful price I had to pay for abandoning him first.

When Dan died, his illuminating proof of my own inner light died, too. I became unrelentingly hungry for love and validation. Brutalized by loss, I spent years struggling and striving to find another sustainable light source. Ironically, though, the sacred lessons Dan and his death taught me had nothing to do with external sources—and everything to do with learning how to source myself. I became my own best friend and my own light in the darkness—and, most of all, my own beloved.

Broadening my concept of love so that it did not necessarily require another person, even Dan, has been one of the hardest lessons of my life. Since so much of an unhappy achiever's self-concept is contingent upon outside sources, love becomes less of a gift we give ourselves, than a grand prize earned whenever we do or give away enough to deserve it.

When my therapist presented me with the idea that being *in love* was a state that was always available to me, regardless of whether I was in a relationship or not, it wasn't just revolutionary—it was fucking radical.

Is she seriously saying I can be in love whenever I want to be? With me and my life? Without anyone else's permission or approval? I mused, flabbergasted by both the simplicity and personal potency of this newfound approach.

That perspective was empowering. Leaning into it seemed like liberation from a lifetime of desperation. The notion that love is ours—no matter who we're with, no matter where we are, and no matter what we do—suddenly makes us more than mere recipients. We become our own method and means of love.

We can press a hand to our hearts and whisper, "I love you." We can make a reservation for one at a new restaurant we can't wait to try. We can crack open a bottle of our favorite wine and toast to today. And we can bury our beloveds, befriend ourselves more fully, and honor the beauty of those who've loved us best by building more beautiful lives.

Our beloveds provide precious opportunities to put our Ambers aside. They see through our masks, and the space they allow for our authenticity to shine can seem like the closest any of us can come to unadulterated self-love. That sort of love is not only soul-affirming, but also eternal, defying all manner of death, tragedy, and trauma. It's not something death can compel us to sacrifice, because it never existed outside of the sanctuaries of our own hearts. Belonging and beholden to none but ourselves, we begin to realize that it's always been the extraordinary radiance of our own beings that illuminates our lives, after all. Sometimes, it takes a best friend to help us see it.

CHAPTER 5

Beautiful

Tying our worth to the way we look is the result of an ingenious marketing ploy, especially when the shining examples of how we should look and live are usually unattainable. Unhappy achieving and unhappily obsessing about our bodies is a winning combination for the beauty industry but not for us.

My mother focused more on my brain than my beauty, and I believed this was because she thought I had a better shot at being smart than beautiful.

For most of my life, I didn't think I was beautiful. I felt especially ugly during childhood. My mother made it a point to never tell me I was pretty. Her reasons were valid: She didn't want me to think that being pretty mattered. Instead, she wanted me to focus my energy on grades and sports. Although this made sense, it stood in stark contrast to my mother's strong affinity for aesthetics (as well as her subsequent efforts to help me lose weight). And I couldn't help but worry that her silence regarding my looks was based less on wanting me to be a person of substance and more on a lack that she'd rather not acknowledge.

When we're kids, our worlds are so small. Whether our young hearts wither or flourish hinges on the words and deeds of a small group of people. Every word spoken holds more weight because we hang on to the casual utterances of adults as if they're the ultimate authority. We believe our parents and teachers possess infinite wisdom and answers to the universe's most complex questions. We give undue attention and credence to their every suggestion, drawing unintended conclusions from things mentioned in haste and creating meaning from things left unsaid.

I don't blame my mother for her decision to reserve comment on what she thought when she looked at me. I wonder what she felt about the baby girl she accidentally conceived at twenty years old who was growing up in front of and alongside her at the same time, but her rationale for withholding compliments about the way I looked made sense. Unfortunately, while she remained mum on matters of my appearance for most of my upbringing, the rest of the world didn't.

My wild and unruly curls, my lack of all-American looks, and eventually, my size . . . I let the world convince me that my physical traits were unappealing. And when I looked around me at the women on magazine covers, I knew they were the standard I'd be measured against. Sure, they were older and living lives of glamour, but it was clear to me that was what I needed to live up to. But how? My plan: I would find a famous woman who possessed some of my own features and do my best to emulate the way she presented herself. I picked Mariah Carey.

Mariah Carey was a musical idol of mine, and her star was soaring in the late '90s. *Vision of Love* was the first album I ever bought. I purchased it on cassette tape for a couple of bucks at a garage sale. As I listened to her voice hit the high notes, it seemed like it could travel from her diaphragm to the tops of skyscrapers without effort. The sheer gorgeousness of her sound matched her face on the album cover. She was stunning.

Mariah Carey is a woman of color; I'm not. But, like me, she's a brunette with a full head of curly brown hair. I examined her likeness with the attention of a master baker measuring ingredients. *She has tighter curls,* I thought. *I'll get a perm!* I made an appointment with a local hair stylist my aunt referred me to. The salon consisted of a mirror and swivel chair in the lower level of the stylist's house, but I didn't care. When she turned the chair toward me and signaled for me to sit, I hopped aboard as if I'd just won a free ticket on a flight to become a mini Mariah Carey.

"I have new curl rods I'm going to try on you," the stylist said. I smiled at her with eager anticipation.

For hours, she meticulously wrapped strand after strand of my hair around tight, narrow rods.

Sitting under the hair dryer, I resembled a teenage Medusa, snakes of silver metal consuming my head. I couldn't wait for the big reveal! It took almost as long for her to uncoil the countless rods as it had for her to insert them.

"Alrighty, here we are," she said, spinning me around to see the results.

The sight staring back at me was unfamiliar, but not in the way I had hoped. I had pictured myself emerging from the basement beauty shop with perfectly coiffed curls à la my musical idol. Instead, I stumbled out looking more like Shirley Temple. I felt certain the stylist moonlighted as a magician because she'd somehow managed to make my curls so compact that the length of my hair was no longer midway down my back but just above my shoulders.

I was silent as my aunt drove me home. I contemplated how I'd ended up with such a horrific hairdo, and how I was going to face my classmates on Monday. I tiptoed into my house in shame. My mother had advised me not to get a perm. "Ashley, you already have naturally curly hair. Why would you perm it?" I had ignored her warning and squandered my hard-earned babysitting cash on what might have been the most hideous perm ever inflicted on a person. Now, I was going to have to eat crow. As I attempted to slip into my room unseen, I heard my mother call out from across the hallway, "Well, how did your hair turn out?"

"Dammit," I said under my breath. I turned toward my mother's bedroom to face the maternal firing squad. She was sitting on her bed reading, but she paused long enough to look up and steal a glance in my direction.

"I'm not sure how I feel about it yet," I said, the understatement of the year.

"I warned you not to get a perm," my mother said. It wasn't exactly the reassurance I'd hoped for.

I don't know how long my perm lasted, but I'm sure it was too long. I never got another perm, and I gave up trying to make my hair mimic someone else's. Rather than replicate another person's looks, I turned my attention toward legitimizing my own. And what better way to do so than through one of the most time-tested, tried-and-true methods of rating and ranking feminine allure? Namely, the beauty pageant.

When the opportunity to compete in my hometown's Miss Settlers Days pageant presented itself at the beginning of my senior year of high school, I signed up. And so did seventeen other young women I went to school with. It was a record-breaking number of participants for a "scholarship competition" that had been around long enough that my own mother had once been a contestant. Since its inception sometime in the 1970s, I don't think it had changed much. It still proudly featured a swimsuit competition.

The thought of being on display in front of an audience in nothing more than a bathing suit terrified me. If my main reason for wanting to be in the pageant was to prove I was pretty, then of course I wasn't comfortable presenting my bare body parts to an auditorium full of parents and peers. Fear wasn't my friend, but I wasn't about to let it convince me to quit, either. So, I found myself a matronly one-piece that passed pageant-rule muster and shimmied my small-breasted, athletic body into it.

I was never at ease when it came to wearing bathing suits. After you spend your childhood being criticized for your size and shape, it takes a long time before you feel good about your figure. And even when your body starts to look a lot like everyone says it should, it can still feel awkward. It was as if all the criticism of my body had caused me to separate from it. I started to see my body as its own entity apart from the rest of me because it hurt too much to fully inhabit something others considered so inferior. As a result, my body became a perpetual object of rigorous assessment, obsession, and modification, instead of a wondrous, life-generating vessel for my soul.

Despite all this, I won the pageant. I became Miss Settlers Days 2001 for all posterity, while one of my best friends won first runner-up and Miss Congeniality. Brenna was (and still is) congenial in every sense of the word. She is pleasant, fun-loving, and full of warmth and sincerity. She has warm blond hair, sky-blue eyes, and an electric smile.

I didn't possess her winning personality or classic looks, but I was a good speaker. I was unsure of everything I did on that pageant stage except delivering my speech. I didn't perform well when I was speaking off-the-cuff, but Winston Churchill had nothing on me when it came to memorizing words and orating with booming conviction. I never saw our scores, but I felt positive that the only thing that convinced the judges to crown me over Brenna was my speech.

Here I was, a crowned beauty queen, but I felt like a fraud. I had the evidence I'd hoped for, but it wasn't enough to undo nearly two decades of programming. It didn't stop me from developing bulimia and anorexia one year later. It didn't boost my self-esteem enough to stop tolerating destructive dating relationships. And it didn't help me remember that regardless of what I looked like, I deserved love and respect.

Tying our worth to the way we look is the result of an ingenious marketing ploy, especially when the shining examples of how we should look and live are usually unattainable. Unhappy achieving and unhappily obsessing about our bodies is a winning combination for the beauty industry but not for us.

Idealizing the looks of girls who are not much older than eighteen and constantly shifting beauty standards keep us in a continual state of never-enough consumerism. It's impossible to achieve the type of beauty that appeases everyone, and the process of aging means ever-diminishing returns. So, why not throw in the towel, tap out of this tired game; break the bullshit shackles of buying *beauty;* and appear in whatever manner appeals to our own unique, splendid, and specialized sensibilities?

It took me a long time to stop chasing the beauty standards presented in magazine articles, makeup tutorials, and doctors' offices. I spent most of my life dying my hair blond to stand out, only to discover I felt like far more of a standout with the brunette hair I was born with. *Beautiful,* by any definition other than who and what we are, is a dangling carrot never actually meant for our consumption.

It's a mirage.

I'm discarding the definitions of beauty that don't serve me and celebrating the parts and pieces of me where I've decided that beauty resides: My smile. My almond-shaped eyes. My sensitivity. My sexy hips. My courageous, compassionate heart. My curls that bounce with abandon; and my dark, shiny, straightened hair reminiscent of an ancient Egyptian goddess. My physical and emotional strength. My love. My laugh. My sweet soul.

We are the ultimate arbiters of what's beautiful about ourselves. We always were.

This is the key to aesthetic freedom, one that can never be found in a Botox syringe or by fitting into a smaller size. Believing this is magic: It immediately makes everything we ever bought about becoming attractive bullshit. When we refuse to spend another second wondering whether we're unattractive or unworthy, we begin to behold beauty in ourselves in places we never knew existed before. And all of a sudden, we no longer need a mother's praise or magazine-model looks to validate it.

CHAPTER 6

Puking in Parking Lots

It's hard to feel guilty about not telling the truth when the truth was a walking, talking display for all to see. I was a young woman killing herself steadily, methodically, bit by bit, every day. I was hiding the murder weapon, but my body was the evidence.

When I was nineteen years old, I spent a lot of time puking in public parking lots.

I waited until late in the day. That way, the workday commuters would have left, and it would be dark enough to hide what I was doing. I was making myself sick—a dirty secret I quietly tucked away in my psyche. Whenever I ate enough to feel full or too much of the kind of food I deemed "bad," I watched the clock until the time was right to sneak away and expel it.

As I vomited into whatever trash or shopping bag I could find, the smell of stomach acid revolted and soothed me at the same time. The stench was disgusting, but it signaled a mission accomplished.

Puking in parking lots was a physical manifestation of how I felt inside. Empty. Hollow. Bleeding. Broken.

My soul was starving to be loved and seen, so I starved myself. I morphed into a 5 foot 6 and a half inch, 90-pound skeleton. When I first started losing weight during my first year of college, a high school friend I hadn't seen in a while said, "You look great. How are you doing it?"

"Just exercise and healthy eating," I lied.

I thought that was the answer she expected—the correct, acceptable response. The honest answer was less palatable. And for a time, I actually was working out daily and eating "healthy," according to the misguided standards of the early 2000s. It's just that at some point along the way, healthy eating turned into eating nothing at all.

It's hard to feel guilty about not telling the truth when the truth was a walking, talking display for all to see. I was a young woman killing herself steadily, methodically, bit by bit, every day. I was hiding the murder weapon, but my body was the evidence.

This slow suicide never interfered with my performance of life. I was still a college roommate, a straight-A student, a friend, a niece, a granddaughter, a sister, and a daughter. Outside of a handful of brief conversations and casual comments, nobody said much about the fact that I was vanishing in plain sight. When they did, some were genuinely concerned, and others were cruel.

An uncle I didn't see very often saw me at a family gathering and took it upon himself to mutter in a cold, callous voice: "Do you like being that thin?" I knew he wasn't looking for an answer. It was just an opportunity to be gratuitously unkind to the daughter of a brother he didn't like.

Another time, while I was home on Christmas break from school, my mother and I stayed up late watching TV. I laid my head in her lap, and she ran her fingers through my hair in soft, rhythmic strokes. We sat in silence for a while before she whispered: "You're just so small."

I *was* small. I wanted to be. Inside, I'd been small for so long, and it made sense for the outside of me to match. I thought if I could make myself smaller, smaller, smaller, then maybe I could just disappear altogether. I was regurgitating all the childhood trauma, grief, and abuse that made me small. Everything I was told I was too much of: *Too fat. Too spoiled. Too muscular. Too bossy. Too chubby. Too Jewish-looking. Too skinny. Too flat-chested. Too extra. Too shy.*

We tell people they're too much and not enough in direct and indirect ways. We send these messages through media representations of extreme wealth and physical perfection that most can never possess. And we tell them to try for these things by spending time and money on a system set up for them to fail. In return, they devote entire lives and trust funds to chasing made-up, materialistic versions of happiness that serve few if anyone at all.

That's the perpetual treadmill of unhappy achieving. Slaving away in service of and seeking a state we never seem to arrive at, despite sprinting full speed ahead for a lifetime.

All of this plays out on a social stage with a backdrop of cultural scarcity, subtle suggestions that one person being enough signals someone else's inadequacy. The result is a society of people rooted in a place of lack. A place of less than, instead of more. A place of unworthiness, instead of worthiness.

We're born big, but the world makes us shrink. And when we feel small, we start working to make others small, too—intentionally or unintentionally turning into foot soldiers of the same system that broke us. This is true for everyone, but it's particularly acute for young women and girls. We learn that being small is part of being "good." And early on, we realize that the bigger we are, literally and figuratively, the harder the world around us will work to cut us down to size.

For me, during those times alone in vacant parking lots, the only sound I heard was my pain exploding from the depths of my body and my being. It was sufficient to fill bag after bag, night after night. Every time I was told I was too much or not enough, and my voice and suffering were silenced—it all came spewing out in a pile of self-hatred and shame I bundled up neatly and threw away. So no one would ever have to see it. So no one would ever have to see me.

Today, when I think of the young woman I used to be—one struggling to exist while shouldering traumatic grief, penetrating emotional pain, and incessant insecurity—I feel tremendous sadness. She was dying inside and out, and her emaciated form was a desperate scream for a level of love and compassion she craved. Although no one truly seemed to see her at the time, I see her now. I acknowledge her pain every time I allow myself to feel the full depth and breadth of my emotional experience. Every time I set an intention to accept and honor all of my feelings, giving myself the grace to let the fiery energy emanating from my heart burn, breathe, and eventually extinguish itself.

Whatever hard stuff we feel, whenever we feel it: Grief. Sadness. Hopelessness. Loss. Heartbreak. Anger. Resentment. Longing. Fear. These so-called negative emotions are as significant to our lives as the positive ones we strive for. Still, we often repress and avoid them. But whenever we do so, we do ourselves a dire disservice because they persist in our bodies and psyches. They get trapped inside of us without a way out, dimming our spirit, dampening the luminescence of our souls, and coloring our lives in insidious ways.

It's the betrayal by a best friend that makes us suspicious of every subsequent friendship. It's the parent who was incapable of being present that leads us to spend a lifetime seeking attention. And it's the loss of a beloved that leads us to dishonor ourselves in relationships, so no one ever leaves us again.

The tougher emotions aren't only natural and necessary; they're symptoms of a life well lived. There's no loss or grief without some semblance of love and affection. No hopelessness if we haven't once inhabited hope. No fear without an opportunity for faith and courage. No heartbreak without a heart open enough to be touched. We can reframe and redefine parts of our emotional experience to empower us to create healthier relationships with ourselves and others. We can learn to love and trust ourselves enough to embrace the good and the bad of our everyday existence.

We can be brave and alive enough to feel it *all*.

CHAPTER 7

Drunk Drivers

When we're conditioned to be artificial, we can't see ourselves past our pain. We lose sight of our self-esteem and the significance of our precious human lives. We abandon ourselves for a sense of connection. Clinging to people who are bad for us comes more easily.

"Get in the car!"

He was drunk, which made him quicker tempered than usual. My boyfriend and I had only been together for a little while. Despite that, our relationship could have inspired a diary's worth of drama. I can't say what drew him to me. Nevertheless, I know exactly what turned my head his way: He was a proverbial bad boy. And although I was only nineteen years old, I was already growing tired of being so goddamn good.

He smoked at parties. He drank often and to excess. He doled out disrespect with impunity depending on his mood.

After a month or so of seeing each other, I decided to buy him breakfast. I figured it might be fun to surprise him with something small. But when I pulled out the steak-and-egg sandwich I'd picked up from McDonald's, he scowled.

"I don't like steak," he said, pushing the food away.

I couldn't help but wonder whether it was me or the steak that didn't suit him.

Against all advice and any semblance of common sense, I ignored the bad between us for the sake of being in a relationship. Even a dysfunctional relationship was better than no relationship at all. I treated overcoming our issues like a passion project I could execute to perfection. Both of us brought heavy loads of baggage to bear on one another. I carried the traumatic grief of losing Dan, and he shouldered the pain of being abandoned by his mother.

The heaviness of our collective emotional burdens was more than mere attraction or romantic connection could carry. Though we came from different backgrounds, we were both desperate to find the love we lacked. And we filled that void for each other for a while, albeit imperfectly.

Like everyone, both of us were beautiful and messy in equal measure. I was insecure and starving, suffering from anorexia and bulimia; he was moody, immature, and emotionally volatile. The parts we played in the shared drama of our early adulthood were sometimes poignant and profound, and other times profoundly painful. The same complicated soul who saw me through an eating disorder broke glass with his bare hand after a bad fight between us.

Our relationship proved to be an unpredictable roller coaster neither of us could get off. The ups were filled with hopeful dreams and honest intentions. The downs were so stomach turning, they made the whole ride hard for either of us to enjoy.

"Get in the car!" he yelled again. He was losing patience with my indecision.

"I'm not sure you should drive," I managed to say through the increasing tension in my chest. For some reason, it seemed almost inflammatory to suggest that alcohol and operating a car were incompatible and that awareness made me sheepish.

Turning red and with a voice that signaled he was on the verge of leaving without me, he changed his approach from anger to manipulation, uttering words I knew would end our encounter one way or another.

"If you trust me, you'll get in the car."

I hesitated once more before opening the car door in silence and belting myself into the passenger side. As the young man I surrendered my safety to sped through each subsequent city block, time slowed, and silent tears streamed down my cheeks. The way the wind whipped through my open window let me know we were moving at speeds that were illegal at best and fatally fast at worst.

All I could think about was the fact that it only took a second to disregard everything parents and teachers equipped me with to avoid the situation I was in. Nothing I'd learned mattered in that moment. It wasn't about knowing the right answer; it was about not knowing myself.

When we're conditioned to be artificial, we can't see ourselves past our pain. We lose sight of our self-esteem and the significance of our precious human lives. We abandon ourselves for a sense of connection. Clinging to people who are bad for us comes more easily. It's like drinking poison. You know it's killing you, but it delivers some sort of sick reprieve from an existence that otherwise seems shaky, insecure, and insufferable.

My boyfriend and I were toxic together, but toxicity can be intoxicating when who we are is buried by self-loathing and self-destructive behaviors. When we become impossible to perceive behind our masks, we begin to wonder whether we're just unhappy achievers or half-dead. Even painful emotions feel like an improvement over feeling nothing. We might even mistake them for signs of our capacity for love and happiness.

The choice I made to get in the car that night had nothing to do with trusting the guy I was dating and everything to do with not trusting—or valuing—me. I had no sense of inner wholeness, so I convinced myself to accept scraps. To make concessions when it came to my well-being. To sacrifice my safety to feel seen. To tolerate toxicity to be with a boy.

Self-love is not satisfied with scraps. It won't allow us to settle for less than our intrinsic worthiness requires. But when we've never developed the inner resources to nourish ourselves, we roam through life like scavengers. Collecting bits and pieces of relational sustenance, eating what we'd otherwise deem dog shit and calling it delicious.

But we can decide to stop deceiving and demeaning ourselves. We can say no to the people who refuse to respect us. We can decline invitations to social engagements that drain us. We can stop spending time with so-called friends who perpetually harm us. We can reject the idea that we have a biological obligation to let family members mistreat us. We can stop dating with delusions of saving someone.

And we can stop strapping ourselves into sedans with reckless, manipulative men.

CHAPTER 8

Worst-Case Scenarios

I believed the best way to protect myself from pain was to plan on it, as if slicing my skin would make being emotionally stabbed feel less brutal. I was the thief of my own joy.

I wouldn't let myself long for anything good without also planning for the worst.

Before my husband and I even started to try to get pregnant, I was convinced I wouldn't be able to have children. I studied infertility books with the devotion of Plato to Socrates. I had no apparent basis for this conviction, a fact that made my behavior bewildering to the father of my future children.

"Why are you worrying about something that hasn't happened yet?" Aaron asked.

"I just want to be prepared," I said. "If for some reason parenthood doesn't happen for us in the way we want it to, at least I might be able to understand why."

I wanted to be a mother for as long as I could remember. Growing up, I was the matriarch of my own imaginary family of five. I had three children: "Samantha," the American Girl doll whose story was set in the early 1900s; "Lauren," a wrinkly, alien-looking newborn baby doll; and "Emily," an American Girl Bitty Baby. The father of my fictitious family was named John. It wasn't the most original name, but both my father and grandfather were named John. It was the name I thought of when I contemplated men.

Every morning, when my mother woke me up for school, I took care of my "kids." John, despite being invisible to the naked eye, was an impeccable partner. He helped me see our children off to school and daycare. It's easy to have an agreeable partner when their existence is dependent on your imagination. What a perfect recipe for marital bliss!

I don't know when I abandoned my make-believe brood, but I do know that I was a dedicated wife and mother to them for years. Sometime around the age of thirteen, though, it became too uncool to play with dolls, and talking aloud to people who weren't physically present went from endearing to alarming. Just like that, the first family I ever created for myself ceased to be.

For years, domestic fantasies took a back seat to school and starting a career. But as committed as I'd always been to the idea of being a "working woman" like my mother, I never seriously entertained the idea of not having children. Motherhood was always an imperative part of my life plan. And this made the mere prospect that I might encounter problems birthing tiny humans devastating.

Therefore, I believed the best way to protect myself from potential pain was to plan on it, as if slicing my skin would make being emotionally stabbed feel less brutal. I was the thief of my own joy. Before my cup could be filled, I emptied it.

Winding myself up with worst-case scenarios perpetuated my struggle for a greater sense of control over the circumstances, fortunate or unfortunate, of my life. That incessant struggle manifested in the form of neurotic habits, slightly obsessive behaviors that meant safety to me. They were a security blanket knitted from a desperate desire for protection and control in a world that felt dangerous and out of control. My ritualistic practices varied through the years, but they were usually related to some external horror I internalized.

When a family friend was diagnosed with medullary thyroid cancer in his thirties, I started examining my neck every morning after my shower, a morbid routine. Regularly checking myself for signs of cancer was anxiety-inducing, but it didn't make me as nervous as not checking at all. These strange habits helped me believe I could prevent myself from becoming the star of my own tragedy.

Another time, a friend of a friend started experiencing hair thinning, an unfortunate phenomenon she blamed on years of wearing her hair in tight, slicked-back buns. I'd been rocking a severe hairstyle myself for years, a tight, low chignon that I wore most days. It was my chic, five-minute solution to taming my wild, frizzy, curly hair. It made me look properly in charge, which was fitting, since on the inside I was as rigid and tense as my hairstyle.

Seeing another young woman's hair rebel from the pressure of being pulled too taut triggered my vanity and insecurity. I had always maintained a love-hate relationship with my unruly mane. But as someone with more hair than average, I took its capacity to adequately cover my scalp for granted. Balding seemed like one thing I'd never worry about—until I made it one.

The startling revelation that I could cause my own hair loss compelled me to undertake a dedicated course of study regarding the peculiarities and patterns of my tresses. *How much damage have I done?* I wondered. I scrutinized my hairline and cowlick with the attention of an art student studying Van Gogh's *Starry Night*; my head was a canvas, and every follicle and accompanying strand was a brushstroke. Anytime I thought I spotted more blank space than I remembered, I panicked.

Fortunately, I didn't experience hair loss or develop cancer, but I'm certain my good fortune had nothing to do with my obsessive attention. These practices didn't make me any less susceptible to suffering; if anything, they increased it. They were merely a means of coping with fear. Life had already proven hurtful and hard, and this was another covert way to manage the reality closing in on me like padded, white walls in the cage of my mind.

I was terrified.

Not only was I troubled by stories of other people's suffering, but I was also still haunted by my own past pain. I made a promise to myself that I wouldn't let it affect me anymore. I'd swallowed it down a long time ago. And although it tasted like stale garbage whenever I expelled the good nourishment of food, I mostly managed to keep it from coming up. Dan's death had planted an enduring seed of doubt and despair that loomed large in the back of my mind, even though I didn't acknowledge it. It was a constant, nagging fear that whatever I grasped for too tightly would one day be taken from me, as if too much happiness would have to be paid for in heartache.

Ours is a culture of denial. We go to great lengths to deny things. Death. Aging. Injustice. Pandemics. Other people's trauma. Our own trauma. Every moment I spent in front of my bathroom mirror looking for evidence of hair loss or signs of cancer meant avoiding confrontation with the parts of me and my past I was too terrified to reckon with. Instead of sorting through all the pain I'd stowed away, I focused on preventing future pain. And as long as I managed to stomach my own emotional waste over and over again, I could believe it wouldn't consume me.

But the closer the time came for my husband and me to start trying for a baby, the more anxious I was. Our love story felt like an old-world fairy tale, full of war, long-distance letters, and secret nuptials. Love at first sight may be a cliché no one wants to hear about, but for two twentysomething Americans brought together by chance in Europe, it was a reality. Aaron's kind eyes, sweet smile, and intellectual prowess meant I could forgive the fact that his name wasn't John.

We weathered twenty-seven months of military deployments before we were finally reunited long enough to start a family. Aaron had survived a helicopter crash in Afghanistan that could've killed him, and I had survived a school shooting in law school. Against serious odds, we made it back to each other.

Rather than rejoicing that we were safe, I took our blessings as evidence that something bad had to happen to balance the scales. The only other time I'd come close to experiencing the kind of love Aaron offered me, it had ended in death—violent, abrupt, tragic death.

Dan's love wasn't the adult romance my husband and I shared. Dan and I were kids, after all. But it was equally unadulterated and wholehearted. It was quiet, often in the background rather than the forefront, yet it was ever-present. Dan's love allowed me to walk the tightrope of childhood with a sense of peace, knowing that no matter what, I always had a soft place to land. When the security I found in Dan's love was gone, grief washed over me, sucked the air out of my lungs, and darkness closed in on me.

My inner light dimmed. I buried the penetrating sorrow and regret I felt from losing Dan good and deep, but repression had repercussions. I started to see life in black and white instead of technicolor. The brightest shade I allowed myself when painting a portrait of my life in my mind from that day forward was gray. Gray was just the right hue for the way I lived, something less severe than black but darker than white. I might never allow myself the brilliance that experiencing life in all its colors could provide, but I promised myself I'd never drown in darkness again.

It wasn't until one day, twenty-four years later, that a friend finally put it in plain terms for me: "You only allow yourself so much joy," she said.

I wanted to deny it, but I knew her words weren't wrong. They were the truth. We recognize truths about ourselves when we hear them, even when we don't necessarily like what we're hearing. When someone is brave enough to be direct and honest without cruelty or criticism, it's a gift.

Revelations are transformative. Sometimes it takes someone shining a spotlight on our lives to move us toward acknowledging things we previously denied. The most powerful paths to healing are often lit by others. Honest, compassionate people can illuminate parts of us we hide, and their wise words voiced with good intentions are like magic mirrors. Their sincerity compels us to finally stare at ourselves long and hard enough to see what's reflected back in ways we couldn't before.

My friend was right. Planning for the worst and spiraling into irrational scenarios was no way to live. It was a ruse. A lie. A decoy. A distraction. It was fear and anxiety cloaked in the virtuous trappings of prudence, planning, and hypervigilance. They were an excuse not to live courageously and wholeheartedly, as if living small would protect me from a world of hurt.

It didn't. Disappointment, despair, and tragedy still broke through my shield of nightmares that never came true. When they did, they materialized in ways I could never have predicted—and hurt just as bad.

The time and energy I spent worrying about things outside my control never protected me from any pain and only added to my suffering. My rituals were, at best, a complete waste of time; and at worst, nothing short of torture. Viewing life through the lens of worst-case scenarios meant I wasn't fully present enough to experience the breathtaking moments and depth of emotion that transform us from plodding along to being fully alive. Anytime I was in the presence of true, overwhelming love or blessings, I tainted them with ugliness.

I didn't know it yet, but healing was the only way out of worst-case scenarios. I would have to confront past traumas head-on to retrain my brain to think that life didn't have to be so dark. That sort of self-imposed color blindness robs us of so much richness. When we stop believing in worst-case scenarios, best-case scenarios come into view. And life starts to seem magical again. We're no longer deprived of happiness and joy. Instead, we drink them in, let our cups pour over, and store the surplus in our hearts, knowing that if the worst should come to pass, our souls have been fortified with enough beauty to weather it.

CHAPTER 9

Sacred Acts

*Acts of unconditional love are the only true legacies most of us
can hope to leave behind. If each of us makes a lasting imprint on one
person's heart, consider what that could do for a planet consumed
by immeasurable pain and suffering.*

Although I spent most of my life longing to be a mother, I spent the
first years of motherhood wishing it away.

Motherhood was an ideal I achieved in the land of make-believe years
before I ever gave birth. For so long, I wondered what my baby would
look like when he arrived, and the sight of his delicate apple cheeks and
cherry-red lips eclipsed my expectations in every possible way.

My pregnancy was relatively smooth, albeit anxiety ridden. From
the day I found out a tiny human was growing inside me, I started worrying I'd lose him. So when Ari's heart rate plummeted several times
during my days-long labor, and blood streamed down my thighs in the
midst of it all, I thought: *Here's the story I've been anticipating, the one
where loving too deeply once again ends in devastating death.*

Thankfully, what I feared most didn't come true. Instead, a healthy
baby boy was born. He was mine, inasmuch as he was made of my genetic
material. I understood that his being, while hatched from my body,
belonged to something far bigger than myself. He was gifted to me to
raise, not to possess. The label *mother* meant I was only a steward of new
life, not the owner of it.

The moment I saw my son Ari, I cried. He was so beautiful. I thought

I'd reached the height of happiness. But whatever euphoria I felt at my baby's long-awaited arrival soon gave way to emptiness. I was grateful for the privilege of being my son's primary caregiver, but I couldn't escape a sense of guilt and shame. What good were all those years of schooling and striving for success if I was just going to squander the prime of my life on changing poopy diapers?

I wondered what all the teachers and mentors who'd supported me and invested in my education and career would think when they heard I left law to be a housewife. And every time I accompanied my husband to an office holiday party, I cringed when someone asked me, "What do you do?" In its most well-meaning form, this question is intended to strike up casual conversations with strangers; in its least, it's the most accepted means of sizing someone up against ourselves.

"I stay home with our son," I'd say, before gazing down at my feet with a sheepish smile, as if taking care of another human being full-time—quite literally keeping them alive—was socially insignificant.

What does it say about a culture when the work of those who assume primary responsibility for other people's lives is worth so little? What does it say about us when we grow up to embody the principle that devoting ourselves to another person's emotional and physical well-being isn't as meaningful as paying bills? It's unsurprising that the caring work most devalued and deemed *de minimis* by our culture is typically associated with traditionally feminine roles. Patriarchy understood that to fully dominate and disempower women, it was imperative to diminish whatever we did.

But carrying children is essential to humanity's survival, and that means it's a superpower. Perhaps this simple truth starts to explain why our reproduction was transformed from a source of strength into a wellspring of weakness. From a biological blessing to a physiological curse. From sexual freedom to strict carnal control.

Even when the likes of Oprah deem motherhood the hardest job, it sounds like little more than a hollow platitude. We may have heard motherhood proclaimed the most important job ad nauseam, but we know the world doesn't buy it. We've been taught to discount any act that isn't provided for public consumption, so we're persuaded that quiet labors of pure love performed in private can never amount to anything of value.

But what if the opposite is true? What if unpaid service work is so critical that capitalism would crumble without it? What if unnoticed acts of compassion and caring are more likely to transform humanity than anything that happens on a public stage? And what if we're only indoctrinated to think otherwise to sustain a system that requires our service be so subservient as to be valueless?

I've heard genuine gestures of care, from childcare to eldercare, referred to as "small acts." And it's true that we're conditioned to consider them insignificant compared to achievements and success, both in terms of scale and effect. Yet such acts of compassion are anything but small—they're sacred.

A world that breeds unhappy achievers brainwashed me to believe that being a caregiver for my baby boy wasn't as blessed or brilliant as being a "big shot" lawyer. But Dan's short life demonstrates the opposite. Dan wasn't famous. He didn't even live long enough to "make a living," let alone answer awkward, obligatory questions about it at dinner parties. I can't say much else about what he did during his brief life. There isn't anything that will make him sound worthy of a posthumous Nobel Prize or Academy Award. However, in less than thirteen years, he left a legacy. It wasn't born out of bestselling books, fame, or a fancy career at a Fortune 500 company. It was born out of love.

Success can never be as soul-nourishing or fulfilling as love, no matter what our society says. Acts of unconditional love are the only true legacies most of us can hope to leave behind. They ripple, regenerate, and endure long after renowned successes and accolades fade, forgotten or buried. If each of us makes a lasting imprint on one person's heart, consider what that could do for a planet consumed by immeasurable pain and suffering.

If we globalize anything, let it be compassion.

When I come home to the sleepy slice of rural Illinois that raised me, I try to carve out time to bring flowers to Dan's grave. I lay fresh, brightly colored blooms down in front of the tombstone that memorializes someone who meant so much to me. The sight of them always moves me to wonder whether there's anything more beautiful than a life remembered long after its end.

I doubt it.

But as I struggle to balance a writing career with a lifelong calling and commitment to be a mother, I sometimes worry whether I have the capacity to do them both without doing one or the other a disservice. They can seem like competing interests that can't coexist as seamlessly as I wish they would. Although they share some commonalities: My children are as miraculous and wondrous to me as well-chosen words. Both imbue days that might otherwise be mundane with meaning. They're both lighthouses leading me home when I'm lost in darkness. They both inspire a purity of love and spirit that makes it impossible to believe our true nature isn't beautiful. They both connect me to an innate innocence that reminds me that creativity is a critical food source for the soul.

Society sees them as anything but the same, despite their similarities. Somehow, words on pages are received with a recognition and reverence that raising the happiest, most well-adjusted humans isn't. Still, the most ardent praise in response to any piece I've ever written can't compare with the wave that washes over my heart when one of my children pulls my face toward theirs, holds my head between the palms of their little hands, and lands the most earnest kiss on my cheek.

No one notices it. No one will ever see it. No one will deem it novel or noteworthy. Yet it's satisfying and sweet in a way the other stuff of life isn't. And that tells me it's more significant than anything else I'll ever do.

Part Two:

Unbecoming

CHAPTER 10

Mothers & Martyrs

We were born to build lives that align with what we see in our dreams. Sacrificing ourselves for others, even our own children, isn't selflessness—it's self-sabotage.

A few years ago, my husband and I considered moving from our home in the Midwest to the East Coast. I told my parents, hoping to have their support, but I may as well have asked them to set their hair on fire. My mother stated without equivocation that when I became a mother, I gave up the right to move away from my extended family. Apparently, I missed this fine print in the birth certificate.

My mother was serious. Relocating anywhere a plane ride away was selfish, she made it clear, and I should remain within driving distance of my hometown for the sake of my kids. What I wanted was secondary at best, and at worst, irrelevant. It didn't matter why we were considering moving, whether there were more professional opportunities, better weather, or easier access to things we enjoy. My mother stated that such a move would constitute a personal offense that wasn't only egregious, but unforgivable.

Although it hurt to hear, I knew my mother was merely applying the same standards of motherhood to me that she appeared to apply to herself.

My mother dropped out of college when she became pregnant with me and married my father. Years later, she returned to school while working full-time and supporting a family. She pored over yellow legal pads and textbooks, highlighting the pertinent parts of undergraduate lectures by lamplight in the dead of night. I felt deep gratitude and admiration for a woman who held hard work dear and instilled the same in me, one who didn't let the responsibilities of marriage and motherhood deprive her of at least one heartfelt dream she had for herself.

Still, somewhere in the choices my mother made, I wouldn't be surprised if she felt like she had to forgo some of her ambitions to do the *right* things for her daughter.

Instead of climbing the corporate ladder and building a career with her business degree, she managed the business of a small dental office for thirty years. She strived and sacrificed to afford me a life like the one that might've been meant for her. The problem was that the life she envisioned for me didn't seem to leave much room for my own vision. The aspirational identity imparted upon me by the woman who raised me wasn't wrong; it just wasn't mine.

All the tireless time and money my parents dedicated to providing for my education was expected to be repaid by pursuing professional degrees, not their daydreaming daughter's passion for the arts. For some reason, lawyering seemed more impressive than literary work to my family, so I never allowed myself to consider any other occupation.

Even a decision as deeply personal as choosing where to live became part of the unspoken, unending quest of my mother's to make a life for me that reflected her ideas and ideals. Whether out of obligation or honest affinity, my mother never moved more than minutes away from *her* mother.

The choice of Marengo, Illinois, was made for me by my mother's parents before I was even born. Motherhood could have made me complicit. It's what mothers are encouraged to do: forget themselves for the sake of future generations. But what are often seen as simple acts of sacrifice and selflessness can be far more insidious and damaging.

Before the controversy over my hypothetical move erupted, I'd never been so blatantly asked to martyr myself for my children. I appreciated that our loved ones were so distraught at the thought of us leaving. Yet there's a difference between being beloved and being confined. Manipulation, fear, or control dressed up in beautiful and genuine feelings are still, ultimately, ugly. When we act solely in their service, we almost always do ourselves and those we hold dear a disservice.

Women are brainwashed to believe that their happiness is the price to pay for being good. Not just good mothers, but good wives and daughters. *Good* is living somewhere someone else says is best. *Good* is studying what someone else says is smart. *Good* is staying in a shitty job because someone else says it's responsible. *Good* is being quiet and fading into the background of every room like a worn-out wall tapestry. *Good* is denying all our soul's callings and innermost knowing to serve the interests of someone other than ourselves. *Good* is living in ways that make us feel more dead than alive so everyone else can remain comfortable and undisturbed.

It's not just men who trap us in these expectations. Countless times, I've seen women police one another back into the narrow, suffocating box of good whenever one tries to escape. Anytime a woman begins to gather enough courage to leave a long-standing marriage for reasons other than outright abuse or infidelity, there's always another woman eager to judge her: "Just because she isn't happy doesn't make it okay to break up a family," she'll say.

Um, excuse me, but yes. Yes, it fucking does. How many people report having benefited from being raised by unhappily married parents?

"I'm so glad my parents stayed in an insufferable marriage for me," said no one, ever. The fact that someone is actively suffering by staying means that the family is already broken. What good are we to those we love if we're stuck, stagnant, and resentful? What would happen if women stopped martyring ourselves under the goddamn guise of good? What would happen to the world we inhabit if we were no longer confined by the false, fucked-up chains of good and claimed liberation, full personhood, and freedom, instead?

We were born to build lives that align with what we see in our dreams. Other people's needs, wants, and feelings are important, but they aren't the only ones that matter. No one wants to be cited as justification for a choice that makes someone else miserable. Sacrificing ourselves for others, even our own children, isn't selflessness—it's self-sabotage.

And I'm realizing that cultivating self-love and creating a life that lights me up, so I can be a brighter beacon in the lives of my children and others, isn't selfishness. It's self-care. Being raised to believe I was responsible for everyone else's feelings and experiences meant that my feelings and experiences didn't matter. If someone was upset, and I was the source, I was wrong. But that wasn't only untrue, it made inner peace and fulfillment impossible by forcing me to surrender all my power to other people. Not understanding that how I experience the world is primarily up to me was like being a ping-pong ball, batted and bounced around by other people's judgments. But making myself the headmistress of my own internal experiences wasn't only empowering—it made martyrdom impossible.

Although all my feelings are allowed, how I interpret and respond to them is my choice. An internal trigger isn't another individual's issue; it's an impetus for my own emotional exploration. It's a problem inside me asking for attention. On the other hand, the fact that a conscious, considered choice I've made for my family makes someone else uncomfortable is just that—a fact, not my fault.

Acknowledging someone's full humanity means accepting and respecting their autonomous right to make choices most resonant for them.

And we, as parents, choose to bear children. The payoff for that choice is the privilege of witnessing the evolution of a beautiful soul from birth to full bloom, making their wobbly way through the world and brimming with the innocence and optimism of a young life yet to unfold. That's our reward. The blessing of being a steward for a spirit some higher power or stroke of biological luck saw fit to bestow upon us is our recompense. Motherhood as a role is a reward unto itself.

It's time to cast off the antiquated idea that our children owe us anything. True love, like that between mother and child, should be selfless and unconditional. But selflessness doesn't mean sacrificing oneself for someone else. It means love for the sake of love, without a personal stake or implied contract to be fulfilled by one's offspring later as compensation for parental services rendered in childhood.

And it might be easier for us as mothers to love our children without expectation if society stopped teaching us that motherhood is the simultaneous experience of the birth of a child and the death of parts of ourselves. We're more likely to allow our children to build lives unencumbered by our "blessings" and expectations when we've afforded ourselves the same grace.

We are not parents first; we are people first. We are not mothers first; we are women first. Our deepest desires are ample justification for altering the course of our lives, irrespective of anyone else's wishes. Love both blesses and compels me to be many things: a wife, a mother, a sister, a daughter, a friend.

And I'll never bastardize love to be a martyr.

CHAPTER 11

Critics & Bait

Critiques of any kind are kryptonite to unhappy achievers: We flex
our muscles from critical acclaim, puff out our chests, and swell with
pride, but we give all our power away to other people. As swiftly as
their approval builds us up, their disapproval destroys us.

I once accepted the cuts of criticism as if every laceration was a biblical verse, a divine declaration of truth I had no choice but to believe.

Compliments, on the other hand, concerned me. I couldn't receive them, and rarely could I even conceive of them. My mind resisted flattering remarks, despite working so hard to earn them. Because my opinion of myself was so low, I was more comfortable absorbing negativity than positivity. A negative comment substantiated my self-critical stories; a positive comment called them into question. I became conditioned to believe every bad thing said about me, while discounting and disregarding any positive thing. Praise blew past me like a gentle wind, felt only for a fleeting second if noticed or acknowledged at all. But harsh words penetrated me like indelible rhetorical bullets, riddling my consciousness and obliterating my confidence.

Fragile self-esteem was a consequence of a childhood in which I was routinely told I was too much. In third grade, I came home from school and cried in my grandmother's arms after a boy declared me to be as "big as an alligator." We were collaborating on a class mural, and he never even looked up from the reptilian creature he was coloring to notice the color draining from my face. Without so much as setting his green marker down, he handed me a memorable lesson in social scrutiny and body shame. Another boy on a bus ride to school told me to "move over, fatass," while family members mentioned how big my belly was in my bathing suit.

In other words, I was chubby. Being chubby meant being too much and not enough at the same time. Inhabiting a body condemned for taking up too much space made me believe I was inadequate and small. This ingrained feeling of inferiority followed me into adulthood.

Early in my writing career, I wrote a few pieces that were published in *Ms.* magazine. Growing up, I had idolized Gloria Steinem, so the idea that my work would be printed in her iconic brainchild was an unbelievable dream. I was thrilled and eager to publish more. Where else could I send my writing?

Since I didn't have professional writing experience or mentors, my godmother offered to connect me with a journalist she knew. The journalist worked for *Slate* magazine, and her father was a friend of my godmother. I'd mostly navigated the literary wilderness alone, so I was excited to meet her.

My excitement turned to dismay, though, when the email that put us in touch included the previous correspondence that transpired to make the introduction possible. In earlier messages exchanged between the journalist and her father, he asked his daughter whether she'd be willing to speak with me. He included a link to one of my op-eds for *Ms.* magazine, and said:

Let her know it's "bated breath," not "baited breath."
Love, Dad

I was mortified. My stomach roiled with silent indignity. It was the sort of feeling I woke up to after a recurring nightmare in which I venture out in public without realizing I'm naked, a dreadful awareness of being unwittingly exposed. Embarrassment kept me from ever contacting that journalist.

Of course, I blamed her father for it.

I decided I didn't like him based on one offhand comment that he probably never meant for me to see. I condemned his daughter for his sin, too. My sensibilities were so delicate that the mere mention of a minor mistake caused me to collapse inside, to shut down and withdraw from an opportunity that might've been invaluable. When your faith in yourself is easily shaken, even constructive feedback feels like an affront. Every unkind or unfavorable remark shreds and fragments your sense of self, as if you were made of papier-mâché instead of flesh and bone.

I continued to write and participate in public discourse despite feeling like an intellectual fraud. My insecurity peaked when I began writing professionally. Convinced that my successes were attributed to luck, and failures were evidence of inferiority, I carried a constant fear of being found out. I wondered what would happen if the fact that I didn't know everything about everything was eventually laid bare. I assumed everyone else somehow knew everything, or at least knew more than I did. It didn't matter how many credentials or degrees I accumulated or how many people applauded my work, nothing and no one could convince me of my own adequacy.

Existing is exponentially more difficult when you're so vulnerable to the opinions of others. I spent a lifetime using achievement, perfection, and kindness to avoid criticism. Critiques of any kind are kryptonite to unhappy achievers: We flex our muscles from critical acclaim, puff out our chests, and swell with pride. But this sense of satisfaction is surface-level and unfulfilling, because we give all our power away to other people. And as swiftly as their approval builds us up, their disapproval destroys us.

Eventually, I learned that no one needs to be an expert to hold notable perspectives. That being too big for a boy at school didn't mean I was too much (or too little). That some critics are teachers with lessons I'm meant to learn, and others are cowards using disapproval to distract from their own unhappiness. That I'd be perpetually scarred and burned by other people's perceptions until I owned myself and my authority. That I had a right to take up space. That it was safe to be seen for who I was. That who I was was more than adequate.

And that risking making mistakes is the only real means of living a meaningful life.

CHAPTER 12

Good Grief

The shadow of that love was the single source of all my suffering.
It poured out of me in precious waves of pain. Electric currents of
heartbreak reverberated through me until being in my body became an
affliction, and I wished my soul could shed it for a second of solace.

"**A**re you here to talk to the dead?"
The question stunned me like a swift blow to the back of the head. "Uh, well," I stammered, responding to the tattooed stranger staring at me from across the table. "I guess I'm just here for whatever you offer."

Not a reply I'd typically give to a man I'd just met. The real answer was that it never occurred to me that connecting with the deceased was an option, and I was intrigued.

Aaron and I were celebrating my thirty-seventh birthday with a romantic weekend getaway in Galena, Illinois. It wasn't my first choice for our destination. I would have preferred a more urban setting like Chicago, but that simply wasn't possible in a pandemic. I'm not entirely sure what inspired Aaron to suggest we steal away to that small city in the rural, rolling landscape of northwest Illinois, but it was sweet. Known for its nineteenth-century architectural charm, and the site of a historical home of Ulysses S. Grant, Galena is a little gem in the Midwest.

After a day of wine tasting and meandering through quaint city streets, I suggested we wander into the medium's shop, looking for nothing more than a Saturday-night amusement. There I was, sitting in front of a medium named Christopher, unsure whether to take him up on his offer to speak to someone six feet under. He sensed my hesitation. "If not, that's all right," he said. "I'm just getting a sense of what you're here for."

I was starting to wonder the same thing.

But then he delivered a twenty-minute reading so accurate it made my husband think he must've found an unauthorized biography about me. He knew details about my life, and the people in it, that I'd never shared with anyone before. And his assessment of the state of my life—outwardly beautiful, inwardly broken—couldn't have been more accurate. I was astounded, and we left that night in a state of disbelief.

After returning home, I couldn't shake the man's question: *Are you here to talk to the dead?* He was right about so many things about me—maybe he was right about that, too. Had I been there to talk to the dead?

Or was a spirit asking to speak with me?

Death isn't a subject people typically care to discuss, but for me it was taboo. I'd been running from Dan's death for decades, so I avoided anything that made me grapple with mortality.

The terror of that loss stuck with me. I could still see myself sitting at my family's breakfast table eating cereal on a sunny Saturday morning in August when the phone rang. A few minutes later, my mother entered the kitchen and said: "Ashley, Dan died last night." I sat, frozen in my seat for a second, my body absorbing a blow my mind didn't know how to. Unable to form a single sentence, I set my cereal bowl down in silence, marched to my bedroom in a zombie-like stupor, locked the door, and fell to the floor.

That was the moment my childhood ended.

The reality that Dan was dead gutted me from the inside out. It was as if one of the deepest, most vital parts of me had been ripped apart and laid bare on an operating table. My soul bled, and I couldn't see a clear way to stop the carnage.

Death seemed so cruel and inhuman, and I didn't know how to cope with it. So I didn't; I buried it, instead. Not only did I do my best to avoid talking about Dan or his death, but I also attempted to extinguish his memory altogether. Simply reckoning with the mere fact of his former existence felt like being stabbed in the stomach. Maybe I couldn't force myself to forget him, but I wouldn't volunteer to sit vigil in remembrance of someone whose absence agonized me.

After twenty-four years of suppressing my grief, I'd become remarkably adept at keeping unwanted emotions at bay. I wore my ability to endure hard shit without letting it derail me from daily life like a deranged merit badge of mental fortitude. I believed that surviving the traumatic loss of someone I loved showed I could handle anything. Yet, survival implies a continuation of life or existence by overcoming a trying or terrible situation. Is overcoming the same as burying? Could I claim to have survived something I'd never allowed myself to feel? After Dan died, I still managed to exist. But I can't say for certain whether my disconnected, detached state of being was living.

Eventually, weeks of listening to my brain replay the medium's words compelled me to take a chance.

"I think I'm going to set up a phone appointment with that psychic we saw in Galena," I told Aaron.

"Really?" Aaron asked. "Why?"

"I've been thinking about how he asked me if I was there to talk to the dead, and I wonder if I could connect with my friend Dan, the one who died when I was a kid," I said, trying to sound casual.

Aaron raised his eyebrows and gave a slight nod before signing off on my plan. "Cool. See what happens," he said.

I'd expected my desire to connect with Dan to surprise Aaron. I'd only mentioned him once or twice, and conversations about him were brief. I couldn't convey deep truths about us because it would have required me to venture into inner territory that I deemed too dangerous.

Making the determination to call the medium and connect with Dan came easily, but the aftermath of that decision did not. The psychic couldn't tell me anything my heart didn't already know. But the mere act of bringing that lost love to light sent years of buried grief boiling to the surface of my psyche.

"I feel crazy. I'm mourning Dan as if he died yesterday!" I confessed to my therapist. "What's wrong with me?"

"Nothing's wrong with you, Ashley," she said. "It doesn't matter whether it's been twenty-four years or two days since Dan died. Grief doesn't disappear just because we don't deal with it."

It was time to face what I feared for so long. It wasn't Dan's death I'd been denying, but his love.

The shadow of that love was the single source of all my suffering. It poured out of me in precious waves of pain. Electric currents of heartbreak reverberated through me until being in my body became an affliction, and I wished my soul could shed it for a second of solace.

Inhabiting grief meant not only confronting past trauma but also revealing and reconnecting with lost love. Somehow, the more I waded through my own darkness, the more I felt that foregone feeling of sunlight on my face. Because when I buried my grief at thirteen, I buried myself. The emotional armor I piled over my pain made that part of me impenetrable. However, it also made it impossible to be unguarded. All aspects of my existence became even more obstructed than before: Who I was. How I felt. What I felt. What I said. What I did. Nothing about me flowed unencumbered. My emotional armor was a fortress for my heart. Not much made it inside, and even less made it out.

Grief in its fullest form began to dismantle my defenses. It forced me back down on the floor to gather the strength to learn how to stand in truth and authenticity. Night precedes the dawn of a new day, after all. And being broken apart by grief was the beautiful, brutal initiation necessary to "unbecome" an unhappy achiever. It was the cataclysmic catalyst that called me home to myself, again.

CHAPTER 13

Matrimony & Acrimony

When two people are bound together by individual states of broken-
ness, one person's healing can upset the balance between them. Coming
home to wholeness pokes holes in an already porous marriage.

The foundation of my marriage was codependency. The more grief brought me back to myself, the more the ground beneath me and the man I loved crumbled.

The parts of a marriage that aren't working aren't always obvious. Often, the demands of daily life allow the problems between two people to lie dormant. We think only cataclysmic events cause marital bliss to devolve into discord. Infidelity. Abuse. Addiction. But rather than an atomic bomb blowing up a happy home, sometimes holy matrimony descends into acrimony in a fashion more like a beloved sweater beginning to pill or the hem of well-worn pants fraying with each wear. And when that's how a marriage begins to unravel, subtle yet serious problems go unspoken and unseen until something unexpected exposes them.

The buried love that grief brought to the forefront of my brain had been creating a simmering tension between Aaron and me for months. Then, one night, after a powerful dream about Dan woke me up, it boiled over.

"I used to believe you couldn't burn for me or anyone else like that," Aaron said. "But now, I'm watching you burn for someone. You're burning for him!"

"Well, what the fuck do you want me to do?" I cried. "Bury him again? He's already dead!" I curled up in a corner of our bed as rage and heaving sobs hurtled through my body. I felt like a wild animal, cornered, and caged.

"I hate you!" I shouted. "I hate you for condemning me for something I can't change, I hate you!"

We were engaged in the biggest battle of our thirteen-year marriage, and it wasn't a war of wills as much as a bludgeoning of hearts. Mine was pulsating with grief, pain, and lost love. His was shattered by an awareness that the level of love revived within me was one he'd neither witnessed nor received.

Aaron was stunned. And I was ashamed. Grief set my body on fire, riddled my physical and emotional being with boundless suffering, such that the momentary thought of slicing my wrists seemed like it would be a reprieve. I envisioned blood flowing from my body and wondered if the intense pressure of my pain would ease as each pint of blood poured out.

I suddenly understood why it had been necessary to cut myself off from grief at thirteen years old. Without the emotional wherewithal to weather the storm of suffering swirling inside me, it would have overwhelmed me, sweeping me up like a tsunami and carrying me off to sea. If it hadn't caused me to take my own young life before it had even begun, it would have caused me to steadily self-destruct until a doorway to death opened for me.

Aaron and I were arguing about a dead person. But that wasn't the point; Dan was never the problem. The problem was that there were parts of our marriage that weren't working, parts of "us" that weren't fully functional, and facets of myself I'd forsaken. It took the resurrection of grief for a life lost long ago to recognize that our relationship was dying. We could no longer disregard the signs of our impending matrimonial demise.

The symptoms of the insidious sickness between us had been

worsening for a while. Sex became an act of obligation instead of passion, romance, or intimacy. I wasn't excited about sex in the first place. I'd never prioritized my pleasure, and I saw my sexual satisfaction as secondary to my partner's. I loved my husband, but somewhere along the line, I stopped desiring him in the way I once had. I saw my role as his wife as another item on the to-do list. But as with every other role I took on, I was left empty and unfulfilled because I'd poured every ounce of myself into someone or something outside of me.

That's the nature of relationships formed in codependency and insecure attachments. The needs and well-being of others—husbands, children, friends, family—come before, and often at the expense of, our own. We do and do and do for them to our detriment. And in exchange, we enjoy a shallow sense of love and security. We give our all so that the people we prize above ourselves won't abandon or betray us. In doing so, we lose sight of where all those extensions of us end, and we begin.

When we exist only as extensions of others, we eventually cease to exist at all.

I wasn't reawakening to grief or the forgotten love of a fated sweetheart; I was reawakening to myself. I was recalling who I was before my life became about everybody but me. I began to recollect and reconstruct myself, gathering all the parts and pieces of me into a mosaic cobbled together from beach glass. A sense of self shattered by so many years spent struggling to stave off the after-effects of trauma, and surviving solely on the subsistence of others, is foggy, weathered, and worn. So, it takes time to rediscover and reassemble it in a way that renders us recognizable to ourselves again. It takes patience and persistence to bring all these fragmented bits of ourselves back home.

When two people are bound together by individual states of brokenness, one person's healing can upset the balance between them. Coming home to wholeness pokes holes in an already porous marriage. The more I found myself, the more the *me* my husband recognized became a memory, a figment of his imagination. The more I reacquainted with myself, the more my marriage seemed founded on mutual convenience. It probably still appeared perfect, but behind closed doors, it was far from that.

That night, as our fight reached a fever pitch, Aaron and I realized that neither of us was ready nor willing to let go of the familiarity of the family we'd forged together for so long. So instead of stepping into the sad truths we were starting to see, we set down the swords of emotion we had spent all night swinging at each other. We recommitted ourselves to making our marriage work. And we went to bed hoping that a once-holy state of matrimony would somehow survive the acrimony between us.

CHAPTER 14

Selah

———

The salvation I was looking for, the antidote to the pain moving through me like a river that had been dammed for too long, was waiting for me somewhere in the silence of selah. Growth, change, and healing weren't ends I could force, muscle, or run toward, but states of being.

Surrendering to a sea of grief taught me that life happens mostly in moments of pause.

Slowing down enough to pause was completely incompatible with the frenetic energy I used to inhabit. Everything about me moved fast: my mind, my body, my spirit. I was Lin-Manuel Miranda's *Hamilton*, writing like I was running out of time. I didn't talk much about it, but there was a loud, constant clock ticking in my head. I was a walking billboard for "YOLO." If I only lived once, my time to *do* was finite, and every birthday was an unhappy achiever's unwelcome reminder that there was one less year left to do it all.

When grief ripped me out of the mental trance of manic doing, it hit me like a blast of blunt-force trauma. I'd been sprinting through life at full speed until it knocked me down in one brutal, unrelenting blow. I went from racing around to lying on the ground overnight. Hopeless and flailing, I searched for anyone or anything to help me get back up and stop me from falling further into the depths of my inner darkness. I turned to family and friends for advice, but no one had a magical lifeline. No one knew how to save me.

Then I stumbled upon a book called *Bearing the Unbearable* by Joanne Cacciatore, PhD. It was a therapeutic bible for my bleeding heart. The words on its pages gave voice to an experience I couldn't accurately articulate and made it universal in a way that eased some of my feelings of loneliness and isolation. Dr. Cacciatore's book meant so much to me that I was compelled to check out her website to learn more. In doing so, I noticed that the term *selah* appeared throughout her work.

Selah is a word that appears several times in the Hebrew Bible after verses in the book of Psalms. Although its meaning isn't definitively known, it's believed that it could've marked a musical break or interlude, been an instruction to readers to stop and listen, or denoted a blessing.

I decided to email Dr. Cacciatore to ask what selah meant to her, and why she thought it was relevant to grief. I was nervous and reluctant to send a note to a stranger. Despite being an avid reader and writer, I'd never been moved to reach out to an author before. But for some reason, I was stuck on selah, and I needed someone to solve its mystery for me. I typed whatever semicoherent message I could muster and hit *Send* before I had time to change my mind.

Almost immediately, Dr. Cacciatore responded:

> *I'm so sorry about your Dan and the journey that brought you to grief in its full form*
>
> *For us, the Selah Carefarm and its use are related to a few postulations around the word's etymology. First, the pause and reflection. Second, the reference to the word as an emphatic joining in agreement, as a weight, and as a truth. Basically, all the mysteries of the word's origins, and all its nuanced roots, felt relevant to the work of grief.*

Grief is selah, I thought, after reading Dr. Cacciatore's reply. It's the breath, the beat, the musical rest that loving someone lost to death forces us to take. And it's a truth, a gospel of light we're brought to bear witness to in the darkest of ways. In my lowest waking hours, the moments I was bottomed out and groundless, stuck in muck from a past I could no longer ignore or deny—it was quiet. I was still. And that's where I found selah for the first time.

Time halted and became of no consequence to me. Where I was going was irrelevant compared to where I was. All the thriving and striving of unhappy achieving suddenly ceased, and surviving one day to the next was the most I could ask of myself. Breathing and being were the best I could do at my worst.

I began to sit in silence, less out of a deliberate desire to meditate than an awareness that I was too emotionally incapacitated to do anything else. I started journaling as a means to express and process the intense feelings swirling inside me. And I took walks in nature, relying on the living landscape to reconnect with my own life force. Physical movement helped me gain emotional clarity. The expansiveness of the outdoors provided space for healing. Before then, I never saw the value in anything other than doing. I'd never taken time to truly stop, to pause, to reflect. It hadn't occurred to me that sometimes the most nourishing gift we can give ourselves to survive life's harshest storms is just to let ourselves be.

The salvation I was looking for, the antidote to the pain moving through me like a river that had been dammed for too long, was waiting for me somewhere in the silence of *selah*. Growth, change, and healing weren't ends I could force, muscle, or run toward, but states of being. No manner or form of hustling would have made them mine. It's why we don't pray on our feet; we get down on our knees. We lower ourselves so we may be exalted.

Peaceful moments of pause allow us to reconnect with ourselves, our essence, and our core nature composed of love. When we slow down enough to sense it, we start to feel into our own wellspring of divine beauty and wisdom. Somewhere in the depths of despair, we learn to surrender long enough to stop forcing our way through life. And life starts flowing through us again—like a prayer.

That silent inner stirring. That sacred state of letting go. That free fall into everything and nothing. That place where excruciating pain gives way to eternal love. That space our souls inhabit in our hearts.

That's *selah*.

CHAPTER 15

Seats & Seas

When we find ourselves wayward and writhing against currents of sorrow and suffering, the most lifesaving measure we can take is to seek out those who've withstood similar tides. The angels among us willing to carve out sacred space—and love us long enough—for us to see ourselves through the storms.

No one wants to sit at the table of soul-level loss. My friend Kerri and I met about nine months before my chance encounter with that psychic medium sent me spiraling into grief. If there's such a thing as universal order, compassionate people put in our path to move us past our pain are evidence of this. They're life preservers, seeing our sorrow in ways it seems no one else can, grasping our hands before we go all the way under, and saying, "You're sinking in something I understand, but my being here proves you don't have to drown. Let me show you how to swim in this sea."

Kerri's been one of those people for me. She's a widow, a woman who lost her spouse and soulmate much sooner than either of them expected. So, when a sea of grief started to consume me, and no one else could help, Kerri seemed like someone who might understand.

Yes, our stories were dissimilar. Kerri lost a partner; I lost a childhood sweetheart. But I was acutely aware that the differences between the deaths that devastated us weren't as significant as the aching we shared in their wake.

The ache is the longing that never leaves. It's the part of you that was laid open the day death knocked on your door. At first, it's a gaping wound you walk around with, bleeding out in every encounter with a world that doesn't understand why you won't just hurry up, apply pressure, and scab over already. The bleeding stops eventually—either because you buried grief in booze, denial, or all manner of avoidance mechanisms—or because you inhabited it long enough to let the internal pressure subside.

But heartsick or healed, broken or whole, the ache endures. It's the common thread connecting every one of us who's experienced loss on the deepest levels of despair. The ones for whom a phone call, a diagnosis, an accident, or a doorbell ring mark ineffable moments that made us who we are. The era of our existence just before a brutalizing loss compelled us to close our hearts, hide ourselves behind protective masks, and use unhappy achieving to circumvent soul-crushing suffering.

One day we're walking around wondering how people survive the tragedies we see on the news, and the next, the news of the day becomes the sorrow saturating every cell of our being. Suddenly, we're struggling to stay afloat in a sea we never saw coming, and to sit at a table of suffering in a place we never reserved for ourselves. We know we're the only ones we can save now, and that the seat held for us is ours whether we want it or not. We don't want it, after all. No one communing there came of their own volition. Death called them there against their will. Death made their reservation some months, years, minutes, or seconds before.

When we find ourselves wayward and writhing against currents of sorrow and suffering, the most lifesaving measure we can take is to seek out those who've withstood similar tides. The angels among us willing to carve out sacred space—and love us long enough—for us to see ourselves through the storms.

Kerri ushered me through a particularly stormy day during the saturating sadness of my grief. I'm not an expert on grief or its stages, but a few hours before Kerri and I planned to meet for lunch, my emotions seemed to shift from expansive sorrow to seething anger. Aaron and I weren't in a good place, and I had no one other than Kerri and my therapist to hold space for my experience. It seemed like my life's worst loss was mucking up my marriage and making me feel misunderstood by almost everyone around me.

Driving to the restaurant, something inside me snapped. I slammed my hands against the steering wheel and screamed, "Dammit, Dan! Why did you do this to me? Why did you leave me? What the fuck am I supposed to do with all this shit now? It's ruining my life!" Rage soon gave way to tears, but when I arrived, I swallowed whatever was welling up inside of me, ran a tissue beneath my eyes to set my black eyeliner back into place, and pulled myself together.

I don't know if Kerri could see how much I struggled during the couple of hours we spent catching up. But I do know that being with her at that moment was a miracle balm for my burning soul. I asked her how she managed after her beloved's death, what helped her. Mostly, I was hoping for a magic elixir to make my pain go away and settle the maelstrom swirling inside of me. She offered some meaningful suggestions, but no remedy could relieve me of the waves of pain until they receded.

Heading home from the restaurant, I realized how reassuring it was to see Kerri. I felt tremendous gratitude for the gift of her compassionate presence. I was reflecting on how fortunate I was that my lunch with Kerri coincided with my spontaneous emotional rupture—when something unexpected made me stop my car.

I wasn't far from my house when suddenly, without warning, dozens of deer surrounded me. I'd lived in my suburban neighborhood for six years and had never seen more than a lone deer or maybe two. I sat in my car, stunned by the creatures staring at me, feeling a wave of warm energy that wrapped itself around me like an embrace. I wept in my car until the deer cleared the way for me to continue down the road toward home.

Whenever I meet or hear of someone with a seat at the table of love and traumatic loss, I picture Kerri and me. We're sitting at a table with three chairs. Two are occupied by us, and one is waiting for its reluctant recipient to reconcile their place in it. I envision a human humbled by the unimaginable making their way over to the spot we've held for them. They walk in, eyes weary and a head so heavy their neck can barely hold it. Emotional pain and exhaustion radiate from their body like sunbeams bouncing off silver.

Still, we don't withdraw.

We don't coerce them to stay and take their seat if they aren't yet ready. We don't offer them new perspectives, suggest their suffering is part of a plan, or force them to swallow it so we can feel better about being in their presence. Instead, once they've found their way to our table, we stand up before they have a chance to sit, surround them in the arms of a sincere hug, and whisper:

Dear One,
We're so sorry you're here.
But we'll be with you until you're strong enough to swim in this sea.
Withstand its waves.
Survive its squalls.
And take shelter in your seat at our table.
Of solace.

CHAPTER 16

Midwestern Nice

_To rage, to weep, to be in a body that aches with so much emotional
anguish you wish you could step outside of it for a moment of respite.
These states of being are more than just pyres on which we incinerate
whatever no longer serves us. They're sacred altars of growth, empathy,
understanding, compassion, and wisdom._

"**B**itch!"

The lady was shouting at the woman behind the deli counter.

I was ten years old, shopping in my hometown grocery store with
a relative, when I first saw someone cursed at in real time. I'd heard
my parents say all manner of swear words, and I'd overheard ques-
tionable language in some movies they watched. But I'd never seen
anyone outright explode on a stranger before. I found it equal parts
refreshing and disturbing.

Growing up in the Midwest, raw emotion and authenticity are about
as rare as a UFO sighting. We're culturally conditioned to be polite and
even-keeled. Publicly, we smile and nod, feigning sincerity. Privately,
we're emotionally repressed and prone to either withdraw or violently
erupt whenever feelings escape the inner cages we create around them
and rise to the surface.

We take comfort in the steadiness expected of one another. It provides stability and security by eliminating the uncertainty and unpre-
dictability of a full spectrum of feelings. "How are you?" is a polite
question used to greet strangers and check in with close friends. The

requisite answer is often, "Fine, thank you," or some variation. Should anyone respond with so much as a "Eh" or a "Not so great," it's enough to send the unsuspecting schmuck who asked the question into an internal spiral.

Midwesterners like things done the way they've always been done. We don't like our boats rocked, and we favor inconsequential conversations over candor. Which means that managing emotions the Midwestern way is the same as having none at all. It's like taking one long deep breath and holding it for eternity. You can't help being uptight and tense because you're trying so hard not to deflate.

I once had a writing professor who had a therapist who told her that the healthiest lives are the least secretive. My professor lives in New York City, but she's a native Midwesterner, so I imagine the statement startled her as much as it did me. Everything real is a secret in the Midwest. Families spend generations disguising and ignoring the hard stuff that happens to them. Telling stories about parts of myself that aren't easy to look at isn't something most people are accustomed to. It's probably the equivalent of cultural—if not familial—treason.

For most of my life, being "Midwestern nice" made me sick. I was a product of my regional upbringing and indoctrination in many ways: I appeared steady. I acted in accordance with rules of social engagement and generally accepted standards of behavior to an authoritarian degree. I smiled on the outside, regardless of—and often in spite of— my inside.

Excessive politeness isn't the problem. There's nothing inherently wrong with fostering an environment that prioritizes discretion and decorum. It's enjoyable to exist somewhere a courtesy wave is compulsory whenever a fellow driver slows down so you can merge or gestures for you to proceed first at a four-way stop. Civility only becomes an issue when it teaches people to adhere to strict congeniality in situations where feeling sick or sad wouldn't just be more honest, but more understandable.

How can we be human in a place where everyone hides their humanity?

My family and I never really talked about Dan's death. My parents adored him—it would have been impossible for them not to feel tenderness toward a beautiful boy who loved their daughter so well. But after he died, it seemed as if my parents didn't think there was much to say. In the silence of my home, there were hard questions I desperately needed help answering. The most critical one was: *Where the fuck is all this love supposed to go?*

I didn't know how to reckon with or give voice to the tornado of sorrow and regret whirling inside me. To survive such intense agony, I made myself numb. I didn't know what else to do without someone to walk me through my grief. I turned my attention to everyone around me to determine how I was supposed to proceed, and they all looked stoic. So, I figured they must've numbed themselves, too. That was the way to deal with emotions no one can stand to see, I decided. Numb is how we live when feeling too much scares us, so we choose to feel nothing instead.

I survived the surprise thirteenth birthday party my parents threw for me the day I found out Dan died by going numb. It's hard to watch the home movie of me walking up to a community park pavilion full of family and friends, all eagerly awaiting my arrival. I'm smiling, of course. That's what I knew to do. The only sign my birthday wasn't as joyful as everyone was pretending comes when my father, who was behind the camera, said: "That's one sad baby girl today. That's one sad baby girl."

My father was right. I was the saddest I'd ever been. And still it didn't occur to anyone to ask me how I was feeling.

I could have shared my true feelings when I returned to school the day after Dan's funeral, but I didn't. A few teachers invited the students to talk about Dan, a classmate and friend who'd been with us since preschool. There were only twenty-one kids in our seventh-grade class, and nearly all of us had been together since the beginning of our elementary education. I was solemn and didn't speak a word.

I stayed quiet in part because I didn't know how to share my grief, but also because I didn't believe I deserved to grieve. I'd distanced myself from Dan before he died, returning neither his phone calls nor his affection, and I told myself that meant I had no right to cry about his absence now. One of my classmates was courageous enough to cry that morning, and her uninhibited display of despair made me want to rage. In that moment, I hated her. I resented her for giving herself a gift I was denied—the relief of authentic emotional expression.

Allowing grief in its fullest form isn't just a means of mourning a death; it's an act of self-love. Surrendering when waves of sadness wash over us cleanses our spirit. Resisting, suppressing, or bottling it up are futile attempts to avoid suffering. In the long term, they make us miserable by requiring us to detach from the tenderness at the root of our pain. Losing touch with our grief means losing touch with our lost love. We become hardened, disengaged from ourselves and others because our capacity to connect is more surface than substance.

Part of the rationale behind Midwestern nice involves sparing people the discomfort of bearing witness to deep hurt. We think we're being considerate by being "strong," according to a definition of strength that's shortsighted and flawed. It's difficult to see others struggle. But being strong means believing we have the capacity to hold space for people around us, even—and especially—when they're at their worst. Being strong means standing beside those we hold dear while they survive fires and face fears—not turning them away from the heat, putting bandages on their wounds and ignoring whatever started their fires in the first place. Being strong means being brave enough to be vulnerable.

Sometimes, love means letting shit burn. Sometimes, burning is the only thing that's real. Sometimes, to live fully we must be free to burn unencumbered. *Grief. Breakups. Loss. Disappointment. Failure. Trauma.* All of these leave us smoldering, but we can burn without being reduced to ashes.

For most of my life, I didn't understand this. I thought if I gave myself permission to grieve the way my thirteen-year-old self desperately needed to, the fire of my pain would consume me. I seriously wondered whether I'd survive it. When I finally let myself burn at thirty-seven years old, it brought me to my knees. I wasn't sure how

I was going to get back up again. But I did. And when I rose from the ashes, I was stronger, clearer, lighter. Parts of myself that I had buried emerged. My heart, clenched and closed, unfurled like a flower. And life looked more beautiful than before.

To rage, to weep, to be in a body that aches with so much emotional anguish you wish you could step outside of it for a moment of respite— these states of being are more than just temporary. They're pyres on which we incinerate whatever no longer serves us. They're sacred altars of growth, empathy, understanding, compassion, and wisdom. They often arise before the best versions of us are born.

But this process isn't only a rebirth. It can also be a remembering, a trigger to refresh our recollection of who we used to be before we let the fear of hurting too much turn us to stone. It's the matchstick that lights the fire of unbecoming, melting away the injuries that compelled us to become unhappy achievers to begin with. Untamed fires aren't predictable, tempered, and neat. Life can be hard, and it's cruel to expect people to be pleasant when burning would be more appropriate. Sometimes, burning is in our best interest. Sometimes, burning is better than extinguishing emotions asking for attention. Sometimes, burning is the bridge between a painful past and a fuller, freer future.

The emotional culture of the Midwest might be nice. But it isn't always *kind*.

CHAPTER 17

Naked & Afraid

Sometimes we must be stripped bare to finally bear witness to our own internal strength. The trappings of survival in a modern world can bury our authenticity; it is a world that may seem crueler and more unforgiving than the natural one from which we originate.

Reality television has been my guilty pleasure for as long as I can remember. Because I spent so many years worried and anxious about the future, watching reality play out in the present was grounding and reassuring.

The first reality TV show I ever saw was *The Real World San Francisco* in 1994. Reality TV was fairly new back then, and I was fascinated by the idea of twentysomething strangers selected to live together in a lavish house in the city. I wasn't more than ten years old, but I knew there was something magical about capturing a life on camera in real time. It mystified and captivated me. And it made me a lifelong reality TV addict, unscrupulously consuming other people's dramas with a comforting sense of "at least it isn't me" as their social conflicts unfolded on-screen. The imperfections of others made mine less glaring. And since I was perpetually imprisoned by self-imposed perfectionism, the boob tube provided a temporary get-out-of-jail-free card. It was like tasting forbidden fruit without getting kicked out of the Garden of Eden. Being vicariously bad felt so goddamn good.

Aaron couldn't understand how his otherwise sophisticated wife could stomach such "smut." But the truth was, I spent so much time stuck in my head that even simple storylines were too stimulating. Incessant overthinking and ruminating were ritualized ways of being for me. I consumed outside sources of information like an addict fiending for a few seconds of escape. I didn't have the capacity to sit still with my own problems, so I kept a conveyor belt of external crap cycling through my psyche. Never mind that this perpetual pattern kept my nervous system overstimulated and anxious. I was an atheist and intellectual, after all. The only way to make sense of my existence was to overanalyze every conceivable fact that made up my everyday life. And so in my downtime, all I wanted to do was tune out.

I vacillated between a state of high analytical performance and a mostly nonverbal, staring stupor when I practiced law. After a day juggling dozens of court cases, trying to discern what *justice* looked like for strangers accused of domestic violence crimes, I'd come home and pour a glass of wine before I even put my briefcase down. Then, I'd slip into sweats and go comatose to television staples like *My 600-Lb. Life* until falling asleep and starting over again. *Reality TV. Rest. Repeat.* I wished for weekends and survived the workweek on a steady diet of alcohol and spying on the people who surfaced on my flat screen.

But the relationship between reality TV and surviving took on new meaning for me during the pandemic. I graduated from classic domestic favorites like *The Real Housewives* to the wide world of outdoor survival. The moment I asked my father what the hell he was watching after a quick side glance at *his* flat screen flashed images of naked humans in hot, barren terrain, I was hooked. *Naked and Afraid* quickly replaced every other series I'd ever seen as the go-to source for my reality programming fix.

Watching people volunteer to forgo every known creature comfort—clothing, indoor plumbing, convenient food sources, personal hygiene amenities, temperature-controlled shelter—to subsist in harsh, unforgiving environments for twenty-one days with nothing but a knife and a cooking pot was mesmerizing. It was equal parts awe-inspiring and cringe-inducing. *Why the fuck would anyone want to do this?* I wondered. Yet every time Jeff, a veteran on the show, slayed another deadly reptile or fish and let out his signature primal scream in celebration, I fell a little bit more in love with the survivalist brand of crazy.

Sleeping near alligator-infested waters and stepping on venomous snakes satisfied my quarantine need for a glimpse of an existence far more interesting than the one I was resigned to within the four walls of my house. It wasn't quite macabre, but it flirted with death. Danger loomed large in every episode. And the longer the cast members lived in the wild, the more untamed they became. To adapt to the elements and withstand ferocious animals, they transformed from civilized to savage, from domesticated to feral. But what was most striking was that even as some descended into primal form, they ascended emotionally.

The personal journey they signed up for was far different in both substance and circumstance from my own. Yet somehow, I could relate. I wasn't in the swamps of New Orleans or an African jungle; I was on my couch. Still, I knew what it was to survive an experience that seems insurmountable. Lions weren't looking me in the eyes, but I was being forced to confront my own inner beasts almost daily. All the defenses that served me well for decades were suddenly gone. And then, there I was, abandoned in the wilds of pain and suffering I could no longer suppress.

Inside, I felt naked and afraid.

Suddenly, survival depended on tending to needs that were so basic I never seriously considered them before. Love, compassion, and acceptance became the healing equivalents of food, water, and warmth. They weren't easy to come by, and all the guidebooks and manuals in the world couldn't prepare me for the challenges of facing my own inner wilderness. I had to search, scrounge, and claw my way to the things that saved me. And more than once, alone in the quiet, open expanse of my existence, I questioned whether I'd even make it out alive.

Sometimes we must be stripped bare to finally bear witness to our own internal strength. The trappings of survival in a modern world can bury our authenticity; it is a world that may seem crueler and more unforgiving than the natural one from which we originate. Peeling back layers of comfort reveals raw truths we might not otherwise see. We dress ourselves up and go about our lives, performing everyday tasks and meeting obligations as though this will earn us the keys to happiness and heaven on earth. Ironically, it is often only after we have survived a traumatic experience that we are finally able to let go of the layers of expectation weighing us down and find our way back to our hearts. Inhabiting hurt humbles us. It destroys our defenses. It can be the only catalyst capable of breaking down the ego's emotional survival mechanisms, so we can rebuild authentic selves.

Maybe naked and afraid is just what we feel right before we finally become safe and whole. Maybe it's our ride out of the desolate desert of unhappy achieving back to the fertile landscape of self-love.

CHAPTER 18

Gossip Girl

*An increased capacity for compassion and a sense of connectedness
to others made it impossible for me to perpetuate my old habit.
Because the less I hurt inside, the less hurt I caused on the outside.
The happier I was with me, the happier I could be for others. The more
I loved myself, the more I favored lifting people up over diminishing
them with secret slights.*

If gossip was a professional sport, I was an all-star athlete.
In my youth, I gossiped more than I care to admit. It was one of
my favorite pastimes to enjoy with my father. Although I won't say I
learned it from him, my father is our family's resident busybody. He
sniffs out a good piece of gossip like a police canine unit smells cocaine.
And he doesn't mean any harm or have a personal investment in what's
said; he just revels in being in the know and enjoys doling out flippant
judgments about other people's lives.

His penchant for talking about other people doesn't make him a bad
person. He's not perfect, but he's pretty great. My father is, and always
has been, one of my favorite humans on the planet. He plays rock 'n' roll
in a four-piece band, but he's a one-man show. People gravitate toward
his electric personality. An adolescent crush of mine once showed up on
my doorstep just to see if my dad was home.

My dad's sense of humor is like a social spotlight, shining all the
attention in every room squarely on him. He'll do anything for a laugh.
To him, placing a fast-food drive-thru order is the perfect occasion to

practice his best Sean Connery impression. And it also just so happens that whenever gossip is on the menu of the day, my father orders it—supersized.

In college, I couldn't wait to come home to my parents' house on holidays or long weekends, curl up, and settle in while my father caught me up on all the juicy news of friends and family in my hometown. We'd chat for hours until our appetites for hearsay and scandal were satisfied.

Talking about other people's problems was a delicious pastime because while I was all up in other people's business, mine suddenly didn't seem so bad. The problem with gossiping wasn't (only) that the subjects of our scrutiny could find out about it. It's that while I was busy devoting precious time and energy to dishing about and dogging on others, I shirked my responsibility to hold up a mirror to myself. It was so easy and cheap to think I knew what was wrong with everyone but me.

It seemed more socially acceptable and encouraged to take an emotional dump on the journeys of others than to walk mine with both feet. Being a hollowed-out unhappy achiever somehow seemed happier while I was busy hating on other people's pain and problems instead of confronting my own. I had no awareness that my judgments and projections had nothing to do with other people and everything to do with me.

I wish I could say these revelations magically manifested in my mind one day. It would have been less heartbreaking to wake up to some miraculous morning epiphany than to find out from a mutual acquaintance that two of my closest friends were talking behind my back, comparing notes and exchanging judgments about things I'd told them in confidence. No one wants to believe those they trusted would betray them for a few minutes of superficial mudslinging, especially when the subject matter is someone's soul-level loss and suppressed grief.

The aspects of my life they were casually discussing weren't frivolous. They weren't limited to catty criticisms like: "Ashley's so full of herself. Who does she think she is?" They were dissecting some of the most sensitive, intimate elements of my life with irreverence. It took me almost four decades to reckon with parts of my past they reduced to conversational fodder.

It's devastating to discover that people you felt were safe were cavalier with your pain.

Often, reflecting on our relationships and encounters with other people is a requisite part of processing past experiences. Recounting interactions and individuals who've impacted us isn't the same as maliciousness or making fun. There's no benevolence in unkind behavior. And when sensitive details of our journey are bestowed upon friends in confidence, discovering they were spoken about in bad faith feels like a stab in the back.

Nevertheless, betrayal can also be a beautiful gift, a critical crossroads of consciousness and a pivotal opportunity to choose a path: be emotionally beholden to other people's opinions and lack of compassion, or find your inner authority and become unencumbered.

Maybe falling victim to disloyalty and fickleness was karma. Regardless, I gave up gossip as a hobby before I ever became the butt of my friends' scuttlebutt. I lost interest in talking about everyone else as soon as I started taking better care of myself. The more I healed old wounds and reconnected with my heart, the less I could stomach hating on and hurling insults at other people's lives.

An increased capacity for compassion and a sense of connectedness to others made it impossible for me to perpetuate my old habit. Because the less I hurt inside, the less hurt I caused on the outside. The happier I was with me, the happier I could be for others. The more I loved myself, the more I favored lifting people up over diminishing them with secret slights.

When we cozy up on our couches and launch nasty-nice attacks on those around us, it's a momentary reprieve from attacking ourselves for not confronting our own misery. Rather than admit we feel too stagnant and stuck to chase the future we desire in our dreams, it's easier to degrade and discredit people who are doing just that. There's no risk (and no reward) in maintaining a status-quo existence.

Talk is cheap, and talking shit only devalues the messenger. Even if we're never called to account for shameful, toxic things we say to tear others down, the damage is done. Our inner and outer voices are meant for love and liberation. When we bastardize them to abuse others for amusement or to protect our own fragile sensibilities, we just become bastards.

Although I've always been my father's daughter, I gave up being his gossip girl when I stopped giving up on myself.

Part Three:

Happy
Achiever

CHAPTER 19

Over-Givers

—

Healthy relationships are like oceans, flowing back and forth
between us in natural, symbiotic rhythms. Oceans are never drained,
never diminished, and never run dry. When we need a cleanse, their
waves wash over us with compassion. And their steady, constant
currents buoy us up whenever we start to sink.

It's easy to give yourself away when you don't think you're worth
much.

Giving always came easy to me. After all, "good girls" grow up to
be "good women," who give and give of themselves to become women
worthy of love—the beloved lifeblood of their families, social circles,
and communities. We're indoctrinated to earn love by generously
sharing our time, talents, and attention. None of this would be a problem if it weren't for the fact that most of us have never been taught
the necessity of receiving. No one told us that what we give is sourced
from an inner well that requires replenishment and rejuvenation.
Regeneration through receiving is mandatory unless we want to run
our entire lives on empty. How can we expect to nourish others without nourishing ourselves?

A good friend once said to me, "You've always had a hard time
accepting love. You still have issues with it now."

Sometimes the simplest statements are the most striking. This was
a deeper truth than I was prepared to hear. It was part of the reason it
took me twenty-four years to visit Dan's grave. Even his most earnest

adolescent love was difficult for me to absorb. Love slips through your hands when you don't know how to hold it. As a child, giving without expectation was second nature for me, but receiving was a struggle. It didn't matter in what manner the love came, whether in the form of kindness, compliments, physical touch, or companionship: I didn't know what to do with it because I didn't believe I was worthy of it.

So, I repelled it, and it bounced off me like a rubber ball hitting hard ground. Love is malleable, movable, and fluid; I was rigid, inflexible, and dense. Giving was possible because it could be measured and controlled in doses I was comfortable with. Receiving proved challenging because I made myself impenetrable to hurt and pain, as well as joy and happiness. It was problematic because it involved letting other people's energy in. And when we're emotionally guarded, energetic barriers become fortresses for our hearts. Receiving demands openness. A heart that's constricted and closed can't allow anything in, least of all love.

Over-givers attract over-takers. If we don't care enough about ourselves to ask anything in return for our affection, there are plenty of people who have no problem accepting it without reciprocating. We might as well walk the streets offering free candy. Some might think it's a little weird for another to offer unlimited sweetness free of charge, but they'll consume it without question because it tastes so fucking good. And hey, what the hell, it's free.

Although such selflessness can, when appropriate and in healthy moderation, be virtuous, it can also be a recipe for perpetual unhappiness, leaving us bitter about the fact that no one seems to match our level of thoughtfulness or reciprocate our good deeds. However, even if they did, we probably wouldn't know how to accept it anyway. The implicit rules of our relationships don't include even exchange. There's no equilibrium in our relationship banks. One party writes checks, the other cashes them, constantly withdrawing without deposits. It's a damn good system for the one cashing checks.

A few weeks after my issues with accepting love were abruptly brought to my attention, I mentioned the revelation to one of my former friends. I told her I was reckoning with what that wisdom meant for me, and how I could become someone capable of both giving and receiving.

She looked perplexed for a minute, then said: "Hmmm . . . really, Ash? I don't think you have problems with love at all. You just give and give and give love!"

Yes, I thought. *And now, I'd like to learn how to invite more in for myself.*

To be righteous means to act in accordance with ethics and morality. It means doing what's fair and just—even when it's hard. Self-righteousness means moral superiority. It's not based on altruism, but egotism. It occurs anytime we believe we're "better than" because our morals and beliefs are preferable to other people's.

Over-giving isn't always righteous. It can be self-righteous, making martyrdom from what would otherwise be well-meaning intentions. It requires us to overextend ourselves—to sacrifice self-care in the service of someone else—resulting in unreasonably high expectations for others that often go unmet. This suffering isn't forced upon us by an insensitive, unfeeling world. It's self-inflicted.

When we fail to serve ourselves first, we serve no one. Focusing all our energy on other people's needs allows us to avoid addressing our own needs. It distracts us from doing our work. It's like we're gardeners, cultivating everyone else's gardens to ensure they're growing and thriving. Meanwhile, our own are overrun by weeds. Neglecting ourselves is a barrier to building healthy relationships.

Healthy relationships are like oceans, flowing back and forth between us in natural, symbiotic rhythms. Oceans are never drained, never diminished, and never run dry. They spring from a supply of sincerity so vast it's sufficient for everyone to draw sustenance from when needed. They bridge the distance between two hearts unencumbered, unrestricted, and unmetered. No contracts. They ebb and flow freely, and their depth shifts organically over time. When we need a cleanse, their waves wash over us with compassion. And their steady, constant currents buoy us up whenever we start to sink.

If our most beautiful relationships could breathe, giving would be the exhale and receiving would be the inhale.

Relationships don't always work this way, of course. There are times when one person needs to receive more than they can give. When the emotional burden on their back becomes so heavy, they need help holding themselves up. However, these periodic imbalances don't impede the flow of the ocean. The individuals involved understand that such inequities are only temporary, and in accordance with the changing tides of each other's existence.

Reciprocity isn't necessarily sameness. What we require to feel safe, seen, and fulfilled in our relationships often differs from person to person. And that's all right, as long as the overall energetic exchange between us is balanced.

When I sought to receive more in my relationships, I altered unspoken agreements between my loved ones and me. I stopped holding so much space for those who wouldn't hold space for me, and I committed more of my energy to those who could meet me in heart-centered connection. Some of these relationships deepened in beautiful ways I didn't think were possible. Some silently fell away. Some ended in betrayal. And new people entered my life, eager to fill the room created by those left behind.

When we revolutionize what our relationships look like and become more discerning about who we're in relationships with, it can be easy to mistake the lack of neediness we notice for a lack of caring or closeness. But desperation isn't connection, no matter how much we convince ourselves otherwise.

My new friendships felt strange at first. They weren't codependent, like many of my past relationships. The energy between us was airy instead of heavy. No one was harried by compulsory obligations or the other's demands. No jealousy. No judgment. No competition. No sizing up or cutting down to size.

Although I'd only known them for a short while, my new friends somehow felt more familiar than those I was estranged from ever did. I could call them for comfort when I was hurting and dance with them when I was dripping with joy. I could confide in them, and they protected my stories, understanding that our stories are too sacred for distortion or disrespect. They didn't seem to care whether I was a lawyer, a writer, or some new iteration or incarnation of Ashley Jordan—they accepted me however I showed up, let me know I was safe, and wrapped me in a warmth that whispered: "Welcome home, my darling."

Today, I'm not an over-giver or an over-taker. Like everyone else, my soul is far too complex to be confined by or distilled down to narrow, limiting terms. I'm not any one thing, nor are the people I choose to be in relationships with now. We're dynamic. We're contradictions. We're magical. We're messy. We're amazing. And we recognize our worthiness, as well as the worthiness of the other.

We don't give ourselves away because we've learned that hollow people with empty cups rarely have much, if anything, meaningful to pour into those closest to them. Our commitment to personal healing and wholeness reminds us to let the waves of our relationships rise and fall, giving and receiving; allowing the in-breaths and out-breaths, fluctuations, and sacred flow of souls journeying together on a shared current to fill us up with lightness, joy, and abundant unconditional love.

CHAPTER 20

Love—
The Four-Letter Word

♡

The simplest antidote to unhappy achieving is unconditional love.
Not so simple, perhaps, but when we reach this state of being, we're no
longer systemically enslaved.

I bought my first self-help book when I was a sophomore in high school. It was called *In the Meantime: Finding Yourself and the Love You Want* by Iyanla Vanzant. Of course, I was very earnest in my belief that the book would help me find the love I so desperately wanted. But the memory of my sixteen-year-old self reading a book about how to change old, unhealthy beliefs and behaviors so I could find the perfect mate seems laughable now. I'm not sure I was even old enough to develop dating patterns, let alone unpack them. Interestingly, though, I met a great guy a few months after reading that book, and we had a lengthy and unusually happy, functional relationship for a pair of teenagers.

Still, I'm struck by the fact that it took me less than two decades on this planet to understand that love, in one form or another, would be the lifeblood of my existence.

I don't just mean romantic love. This is a critical point of clarification in a culture where women are still conditioned to believe that marriage and motherhood are the culminations of femininity. Despite a focus on love in the context of fairy tales and romance, I think my adolescent awareness of the intricate, inextricable link between love and a life worth living went deeper than dating.

After all, Dan had already taught me about soul-level love. I knew the feeling of being loved so completely that it seemed like no matter what came my way, I could be carried through it by a current of care and compassion. I'd also learned the crushing, life-altering lesson of losing it. The absence of love can be just as palpable as its presence. Feeling an absence of love led me to look for it in a book when my life had barely begun.

I displayed external symptoms of this internal scarcity. In high school, I had horrible posture. It was so bad I wondered whether I had some undiagnosed physiological condition that caused it. My shoulders curved forward to such a degree it seemed like an invisible weight was bearing down on my body, as if there were burdens buried inside me so cumbersome I couldn't stand up straight. Maybe I was buckling beneath the pain and grief I struggled to shoulder alone. But I believe it was an outward sign of something more subtle than that: the absolute separation between me and my own heart.

I disconnected from my heart to survive the agony of Dan's death. A person with a heart that's open, fluid, and free isn't afraid to reveal it to the world. Their shoulder blades may practically pinch together behind them as they move through life heart first. On the other hand, a heart that's closed and cut off is more likely to be buried and protected by any means necessary, including distorting the biological vessel that carries it. My body became a cage for my heart, and the harder I tried to deny its pulsating ache in my chest, the more the emptiness caused me to collapse in on myself.

For a culture so consumed by the idea of love, we tend to treat it like a dirty four-letter word. Love is packaged and peddled to us by methods and means so infinite that the slightest utterance of the word itself seems trite. As a result, I shudder at the suggestion that "what the world needs now is love." I will, however, draw from my own early experience of love and loss to propose that if love is the most we can hope to leave behind after our bodies disintegrate into dust, then it shouldn't be among life's least significant considerations.

Nevertheless, a woman who proclaims that love is central to her life's purpose is likely to be dismissed as fast as an early-morning infomercial. If love is the value she dares to lead with, any credibility she might have dissolves. Somewhere along women's long, hard-traveled road to increased rights and opportunities, we were convinced that being treated as full humans meant being men. It was as if some sort of compulsory renunciation of the *inferior* feminine in favor of the *superior* masculine was sold to us as equality.

There's no equality in a mandatory rejection of the most sacred parts of ourselves. Still, we held our noses and swallowed sexist medicine that said that to be taken seriously in a "man's world," we needed to talk like, dress like, dominate like, and behave like them. We based family planning choices and careers on the promise that blind imitation would be the most expedient route to gender equity.

We wore bland suits that obscured our bodies, and our bosses still didn't see us.

We lowered our voices so we didn't sound "shrill," and our bosses still didn't hear us.

We cried when we sent our children to daycare so we could do "real jobs."

We cried when we stayed home to raise our children because we felt guilty and worthless.

We covered parts of ourselves they said were obscene, and still strangers harassed us and aggressors raped us.

We abandoned our ancient history as matriarchal goddesses to worship at the altar of patriarchy's gods.

All this, and still—no salvation from sexism is in sight.

After so many years of forsaking the feminine, I can't help but wonder if we're really so much freer than before, or if an unforeseen price of precious feminist revolution was more unhappy achievers, and further devaluation and annihilation of anything associated with femininity. That's why, although I have the utmost gratitude and reverence for the hard-won victories of feminism, I think it's time for a new term that captures and unequivocally calls for the equal valuation of the feminine and the masculine.

So, I consider myself a feminist. But I also consider myself a *femininist*.

I refuse to breathe the belief that the feminine is less than. I won't ingest and embody this toxic, limiting lie any longer. I won't disavow feminine traits and values, such as love, empathy, and sensitivity, to be taken seriously. Instead, I'll demand to be treated with seriousness and respect as someone who's loving, empathetic, and sensitive—as well as strong, independent, and assertive.

And I'll do so not in service of a culture war of sexist stereotypes, but because for all of us to embrace our full humanity, we must make every aspect of our inner selves mainstream. This isn't purely a question of right versus wrong, light versus dark, insurrection versus inhibition. As we inch closer to an era where gender is accepted as an individual construct to be assumed instead of assigned, and expressed at will rather than prescribed, embracing the feminine is simply part of a larger social revolution.

Although I wouldn't mind being dubbed revolutionary, there's nothing groundbreaking about advocating for the human right to be accepted for who we are. Whether we identify as a man or woman in every traditional sense of the terms or as neither one, we all deserve to be marvelously messy mixtures of gentleness and toughness, humility and confidence, passion and logic—and everything in between.

Putting the so-called feminine back on par with the masculine in the minds of the masses is a tall order. Exposing all the insidious ways being a woman is belittled is easier said than done, especially since we sometimes act as unwitting accomplices in the continued subjugation of our own sex.

A few years ago, I attended a virtual weekend workshop for a women's group run by some friends of mine. They worked on identifying their organization's core values and mission, and I was there mainly to support and observe. One by one, each participant shared what the group meant to her and what she gained by being part of it. It was beautiful to see a circle of women bound together by shared goals, lifting one another up in service of them. As their personal recitations flowed from their mouths like songs, one common thread running through their experiences emerged as the chorus: *love.*

In every unique and nuanced account I listened to, it was clear that love among the members, as well as love for their neighbors, community, state, and country, was what united them as a collaborative collective committed to positive change. It was stunning to witness.

However, when *love* was presented as a choice for one of the group's core values, I was ripped from my reverie. Its suggestion sent shock waves reverberating over Zoom, and it seemed as unnerving to some as a five-alarm fire. "We can't be a group of women publicly espousing love as a central principle. No one will listen to us!" one member said. And without much more debate, it was decided that love wasn't an option.

Observing a forum of women willingly reject love as a core belief startled me. I wondered: *Is this really what equality looks like? Women almost castigating each other at the mere mention of love? For God's sake,* I fumed. *Most of us here are mothers. If we're not brave enough to mobilize for justice behind banners of love, who will be? If universal love isn't our foremost reason for crying out for change, what is?*

It was bad enough that I had been taught as a young woman to question whether something as benign as wearing makeup made me anti-feminist. But now, nearly twenty years later, I was a grown-ass woman being told that promoting love could lessen the legitimacy of my gender.

To be clear, promoting love isn't a priority reserved only for women. A world fraught with fear and anxiety needs love and mercy from every source and all genders. And no one should be conditioned to believe that being a champion of love in all forms and at all times is a bad thing. If we find ourselves bristling anytime love is on the table, we must ask ourselves why.

Perhaps pieces of the indoctrination sold to us were only meant to further subjugate us. Maybe convincing us that traditionally feminine, softer, values like love are lesser was just a cunning way to alienate us from our most potent means of power. If love is our most human legacy, it should be central to whatever we do, especially when we're figuring out how to help the world heal.

We are complicit whenever we reflexively deny and dismiss the feminine in favor of the masculine. One shouldn't be granted automatic precedence over the other. True equality requires a symbiotic balance of both. It requires an equivalent social and cultural openness and acceptance of the feminine, the masculine, and all variations, combinations, and iterations thereof. Only then can we carve out ample space for the full spectrum of individual expression.

The simplest antidote to unhappy achieving is unconditional love. Not so simple, perhaps, but when we reach this state of being, we're no longer systemically enslaved.

Love may technically be a four-letter word, but it doesn't have to be a dirty one. We have the capacity to change it. Not by redefining it but by reclaiming it. We can remind the world that when the feminine was blessed instead of cursed, before everything associated with it was denigrated, before love became a worn-out platitude misappropriated by media marketing, before it was desecrated and demeaned, it was divine.

CHAPTER 21

Enough

We hold the answers we seek. Our internal knowing satisfies
the space inside us that wasn't satisfied before. It fills the previously
unfillable with wholeness and bridges the abyss between
empty longing and soulful liberation.

Quenching my insatiable thirst for external validation was like trying to hold water in my cupped hands. The harder I clenched my fists to keep it from escaping through the cracks between my fingers, the more it slipped away.

I never had enough. I never was enough.

Girlhood and then womanhood represented a perpetual performance. I was doing the show of my life daily. And it didn't matter if I was working toward something impressive or profound or just living. Most often, I was an actress well versed in the roles expected of me. I played the shiny high school cool girl; then the smart, determined young lawyer; next the doting wife and mother; and then, for my encore, a woman striking the perfect balance between work, family, and community engagement as an activist and writer.

It's not to say these roles or my portrayals of them weren't real. I devoted myself to being good at all of them. I desperately wanted to be who or what I was supposed to be. So, I kept looking at, listening to, or scouring every personality, book, article, podcast, email, and social media and blog post to learn what the right version of me should look like. I searched to find a solution to satisfy the incessant ache in my belly. I tried to find the key that would turn off the constant buzzing in my brain, whispering: *There must be more.*

If I could just be a mother, I thought before I became one. *If I could just get published by a big national newspaper,* I told myself before I did. Even after I arrived at a moment of glory that I expected to validate me, I was empty. I had family pictures and professional credentials that looked beautiful framed on a wall, but I felt more unfulfilled than ever.

I always found ways to immediately discount or degrade what I'd done and looked around for the next box to check off on my never-ending list of to-dos.

How could I rescue myself from feeling I was never enough? If I moved from one fixation to the next in pursuit of future satisfaction, wouldn't I be eternally deprived of all the happiness of the here and now?

It was time to stop chasing. There was never going to be that one crowning accomplishment that made my life meaningful, valuable, or just plain worth living. Nothing outside of me held the magic my heart had been seeking for so long. The only one who could fill the void, the long deep chasm in my being that plagued me as soon as I woke up in the morning till I went to bed at night, was me. The road map to actualizing a life that lit me up lived inside me, so I needed to carve out time, space, and stillness to start listening.

Early on in my therapy, my therapist asked me, "What do you feel in your heart?"

Puzzled, the old me had rambled some intellectualized response, hoping that would pacify her.

She wasn't fooled. "No, I'm asking about your *heart*. If you feel into your heart, what does it tell you?" She continued, "Ashley, what do *you* know to be true? You have the capacity to know things, and you can decide what's true for you."

I was dumbfounded.

I didn't know my own heart. I knew where it was in my body. I'd felt it pound in my chest anytime stress, anxiety, or nervousness got the best of me. But I had no idea what it felt like to tap into its wisdom. This realization startled me. The truth was, it had never occurred to me to look to my heart as a source of knowledge.

I spent three years in law school studying how to be critical and analytical. In the realm of law, to make any determination required copious amounts of thought, sometimes to the point of mental obsession and fixation. I believed that external evidence, whether material proof or opinions from people I deemed experts (which was almost anyone other than me), were the only ways to ensure I made the right decision or reached a sound conclusion. Logic and science were my benchmarks. I trusted them to keep me painfully perfect and safe, and to protect me from making mistakes.

But an unintended side effect of this reliance on external evidence was that I lost faith in myself. I stopped believing in my own internal knowing. I forgot that while it's encouraged and advisable to look to credible sources on issues like climate change and a pandemic, I'm the best resource when it comes to intimate details, truths, and decisions about my own life.

The idea that I could look to myself to uncover truth was radical. It was as foreign to me as squeaky Wisconsin cheese curds were to Aaron, a California native, when he moved to the Midwest.

How could I hold so much inner wisdom? Why didn't anyone tell me I could rely on myself to know things, and more importantly, that the things I could rely on myself to know would be the things I needed most?

Even though we all have the capacity to be our own wisest counsel, we discount ourselves. What's worse, we degrade, diminish, and distrust our own internal guides. We let toxic Facebook algorithms, where success is contingent upon comments and likes, dictate whether we're beautiful or worthy of attention. We consume media to determine what's important, what voices deserve to be heard, and what people to emulate. We also look to friends and family, however well intentioned and well meaning, to tell us if what we're thinking and feeling is valid and just. But we are the only ones who know exactly what we're going through and who have all of the knowledge and expertise to apply to our unique experiences.

I started spending some quiet time alone every day, getting to know *me*. I sat in silence, breathed deeply, and allowed whatever arose to arise without judgment. I practiced dropping from my head into my heart, rewiring the broken circuits of my inner wisdom. At first, I could only do this for a few minutes at a time. Meditation was a muscle I had to strengthen. Eventually, I found myself meditating for thirty minutes each morning.

The more I did so, the more I was surprised by what I found. Sometimes the moments of calm were just a wonderful reprieve from the frenetic energy of doing and achieving I ordinarily inhabited. Other times, I had professional epiphanies, such as when the name of an editor I'd never worked with before came to my mind and I reached out to her; an hour later, she agreed to publish my work. Another time, an image of an old boss and mentor I loved, but had lost touch with, appeared in my mind's eye. I soon discovered she had just passed away from breast cancer.

Our knowing isn't always harmonious and life affirming. Sometimes we're given information we never expected. Sometimes we ask questions, and the answers that surface inside of us feel more like hard love than a warm hug. But I've found that even when whatever comes from that deep place of knowing isn't happy, although it may hurt at first, it's always healing and helpful.

In the case of my former mentor, it was devastating to find out she'd died. Yet, I was grateful for the awareness because it gave me the opportunity to write a personal tribute of gratitude and appreciation for all that she'd given me. My knowing taught me it's never too late to say goodbye. And it's never too late to express love and sincere thanks, whether it's just after losing a loved one or decades after the death of a beloved best friend.

The knowing we discover when we stop doing and look inside doesn't just connect us to ourselves; it connects us to each other. The more committed I am to sitting with myself in that quiet space of peace and silence, taking time to turn inward, the more in tune I am with people I care about. There were countless times my knowing compelled me to pick up the phone to call a friend I hadn't spoken to in months, only to hear them say they couldn't believe I was calling because they were going through a hard time or accomplished something amazing and wanted to share it with me. Either way, trusting myself to know expanded my relationships with others as much as it expanded my relationship with myself.

We hold the answers we seek. Our internal knowing satisfies the space inside us that wasn't satisfied before. It fills the previously unfillable with wholeness and bridges the abyss between empty longing and soulful liberation. It's the only real remedy for the constant, crippling call for more. And it teaches us that if we stop trying so hard to hold water, it can flow effortlessly and smoothly through our fingers, as if sourced from an endless well of inner beauty.

Until we learn to look first to ourselves for knowledge, wisdom, counsel, and love, nothing and no one else will ever be enough.

CHAPTER 22

Bleeding

Taking responsibility for ourselves sexually is a sacred aspect of
self-love. It's part of looking after and tending to our internal garden.
The more I experienced and explored sexuality for me, the more I
blossomed from the inside out.

At first, I thought I'd pooped my pants.
Staring down at the unidentifiable reddish-brown substance in my underwear, I was freaked out. *How did I poop my pants without knowing it?* I thought. Then, after a few more moments of peering down at my panties in disbelief, a wave of realization washed over me: I'd gotten my period.

At the strict Lutheran elementary school I attended, menstruation was as mystical as a unicorn, except seeing a unicorn would have been a welcome surprise, and getting my period was not. Menses were something mothers dealt with, and my mother told me she didn't get her first period until eighth grade. I took that to mean I was safe from "the scarlet curse" until at least then, too. But that wasn't the case, and the evidence was right in front of me, or more accurately, underneath me.

I've heard of women who rejoiced in the arrival of their first periods or lamented that they were the last of their friends to start bleeding every month. This was not my experience. Getting my period in sixth grade wasn't just shocking—it was devastating. The parochial education my parents paid for taught me many things; one thing it didn't teach me was sex education. The only instruction I received about sexual health and reproduction was limited to little more than "girls have vaginas," followed by a brief video of a woman birthing a baby out of said vagina.

My mother didn't provide much information, either. She was passionate and open about being pro-choice. Beyond that, though, she was quite prudish about matters pertaining to sex or sex organs. She did, however, equip me with maxi pads and undergarments she referred to as "period pants."

I didn't know it at the time, but my period pants were actually girdles.

I was probably the only twelve-year-old wearing a girdle. The compressive garments kept my oversized sanitary napkins in place, as my mother promised, but the pressure on my abdomen made the bloating and gassiness of menstruation harder to bear. Looking back, period pants were the perfect physical manifestation of the mantra modern women are forced to embrace every month as they fulfill the demands of daily life while bleeding incessantly: suck it up. If men had periods, menstrual leave would probably be a monthly entitlement.

Outside of underwear advice, my mother also gave me the occasional, ominous warning: "If you're old enough to get pregnant, you're old enough to move out." Naturally, I equated unplanned pregnancy with homelessness, a possibility that made pregnancy more petrifying.

That wasn't the only negative association I created around my body's ability to reproduce, and the biological consequences related to it. The primary emotion reverberating through me upon discovering the blood between my legs was shame.

What welled up inside me when I realized I was becoming a woman couldn't have been more inglorious.

I'd seen what happened to other girls in my class who'd gotten their periods. One girl, who was too new to our school to know that periods weren't something to brag about, made the innocent mistake of admitting she'd been having hers for months. An admission that might've been innocuous or even increased her popularity at another school made her the immediate subject of mean-girl gossip and whispers at ours.

Another girl had the unfortunate luck of getting her first period in the middle of PE class. She sat, humiliated, in a pool of blood on the concrete gym floor, while the other kids, mostly girls, smirked and cackled around her. No one did anything to help. She was a pitiful reminder to the rest of us that we could be next. Each day that brought us closer to puberty meant we might find ourselves helplessly bleeding out on a cold floor with no support, and only scowls, jeers, and the sound of our hearts racing in response to palpable indignity.

It didn't have to be that way. What happens to one-half of humanity when their most basic biological functions become inextricably linked to intense personal humiliation, and thus, traumatic pain? What does that teach girls who grow up to be women about themselves and the bodies they inhabit?

It teaches us to hate ourselves.

We're conditioned to suppress, hide, and diminish the most significant symptoms of our greatness. What a calculated, ingenious move patriarchy made when it decided to convince women that their menstruation, the literal and figurative lifeblood of humankind, was a dirty secret.

If—God forbid—a speck of crimson escapes the cotton plug of a tampon or seeps over the edges of maxi pads (often so large and cumbersome they might as well be called diapers) and bleeds through our pants, audaciously exposing itself to the light of day, we fall victim to cringeworthy shame. Shame on her who lacks the requisite care and social consideration to let the secret no one wants to see out.

The world already knows what happens between our legs. After all, the great lengths we go to every month to hide what's happening "down there" are largely due to dictates carefully crafted for millennia to control us. But beyond control, the real power of these precepts lies in the expert ways they've brainwashed women and girls into believing that any sign of their capacity to create life is a scourge on their existence, rather than the most sacred symbol of it.

Our sanctity is ours alone. We can decide whether what happens to us every month is holy or hideous, a blessing or a blemish, consecrated or cursed. If you're like me, transforming your relationship to your most intimate physiological and reproductive processes will be more than a reclamation. It will be your own goddamn sexual revolution.

Revolution requires dismantling—deconstructing decades of indoctrination or, as in my case, parochial education, to expose lies once accepted as inviolable laws. I started to see my period as a sign of health and vitality and learned about cultures that respect and celebrate menstruation. I also read about spiritual groups creating beautiful rituals to *sacralize* monthly cycles, and discovered that in ancient Greece and Egypt, women were believed to be their most intellectually and intuitively powerful while menstruating.

Rethinking my period led me to reconsider my sexuality, a part of me I once thought of as just as filthy as Aunt Flo. Perceiving one aspect of my sexual health as beautiful and empowering enabled me to start recognizing other facets of it in the same way. And suddenly, I was prioritizing my own sexual pleasure like I never had before.

I didn't use a vibrator until I was thirty-seven years old. Orgasming with regularity became a gift I gave myself, and I couldn't believe I'd spent so much of my adult life deprived of something I could've had all along. My sexuality had always been wrapped up in someone else—something I did for whomever I had sex with. If I orgasmed, great. But only if my partner was satisfied was the encounter a success. My satisfaction was secondary, and optional.

Masturbation can be a critical healing modality in a world where women are taught that their sexuality is taboo. Taking responsibility for ourselves sexually is an aspect of self-love. It's part of looking after and tending to our internal garden. The more I experienced and explored sexuality for me, the more I blossomed from the inside out.

Being at home in our bodies, being in harmony with the sensuality and suppleness of ourselves, and climbing interior mountains to reach new peaks of pleasure can provide a path back to parts of us we disconnected and disassociated from because we deemed them dirty, detrimental, forbidden, or simply for someone other than ourselves. My sexuality should never have been for men; it was meant to be mine.

Rejecting the *doing* of unhappy achieving in favor of *being* happy in this world means embracing all of me, including my sexuality and reproduction. It also means being brave enough to question anything or anyone that defines aspects of me in ways that are hurtful or harmful to myself or others. The magic of questions like these is in the asking more than the answering. It's the reason authoritarian leaders demand unquestionable loyalty and allegiance. When we ask, we light the match that sparks the fire of reimagining, empowering us to reenvision not just our periods or sexuality, but ourselves.

What if our periods were hallowed signs of our holiness?

What if they were seen as physical symptoms representing an ethereal balance between the spiritual and the physical, light and dark, heaven and earth?

What if it was a sin for any society to regard menstruation without this kind of requisite reverence?

How would that change the way we see and feel about ourselves; and the ways the rest of the world views, interprets, and responds to us?

And what if menstruation simply affirmed what our souls already know—that our bodies were intended to serve us, not to be weaponized as enduring invitations to sexual mistreatment, suppression, and searing indignity?

I might have mistaken my first period for shit, but I'll no longer accept anything that leads me to regard my body—or my biology—with shame.

CHAPTER 23

Dance

If you want to know your life's purpose, remember what you loved
to do when you were eight. When we were eight, things we did for
fun and play, we did for no reason other than happiness. We had no
agenda, no goals to achieve, no boss on our backs. Whatever we chose to
do, we did with absolute abandon and pleasure.

If life is a dance, I've spent my life as if I were dancing on a stage
everyone could see. I worried so much about how my dancing was
perceived, whether I was interpreting the music correctly, and whether
my moves were cool enough to warrant the title of a good dancer, that
I could rarely silence my self-consciousness long enough to lose myself
in the music.

I love dancing enough to know that the key to good dancing is surrender, letting go to a degree that the music envelops my fast-thinking,
linear mind and becomes all I hear. Once this state of altered awareness is achieved, my body moves effortlessly to the pounding beat of the
tune, taking over until I'm completely consumed. This is *flow*.

Anytime I've been fortunate enough to find the place where my body's
rhythm is in harmony with song, it feels like the closest I can come to
natural ecstasy. The sound transforms into the music of my heart.

For however long this perfect union of movement and melody lasts,
I'm free. The inhibitions I ordinarily wrap around me like armor fall
away, and I'm liberated. My soul longs to be free. It's desperate to move
to a soundtrack much bigger than myself, much brighter and bolder

than the one that normally plays on repeat in my mind. And sometimes in those fleeting moments on a dance floor somewhere, I'm
transcendent.

But, inevitably, the music stops. I remember where I am and who
I am, and I walk off the dance floor. I put my armor back on; invite
Amber to act and interact with the rest of the world on my behalf; and
walk myself back, reel myself in, to that other less free, less authentic,
less soulful (and soul-filled) version of me.

There's a home movie of me at eight years old. My face is beaming with pride because I'm wearing the New Kids on the Block T-shirt
my mother bought me. With a boombox in the background, and my
five-year-old cousin armed with a toy electric guitar, I ask my father
behind the video camera if he's recording. He affirms he is, and I launch
into my best running-man moves.

I dance with confidence at a cadence completely offbeat but
uniquely mine. I know my father is watching, and I want him to. I want
to be seen moving freely to music that lights me up from the inside
out. Self-censoring isn't even in my realm of possibility. I'm dancing,
wild and wrong, and my only concern is making sure my father records
every second of this moment for posterity.

Other than dancing, usually accompanied by singing out of tune
or lip-synching, my eight-year-old self was a storyteller. I was a shy,
introverted kid without many playmates on the sleepy dead-end street
where I grew up. Imagination and creativity filled the empty spaces
of my preadolescent existence. I rode my purple Huffy bike up and
down the steep-sloped road next to my childhood home, and weaved
in and out of neighbors' driveways, making whimsical patterns with
my tire marks.

As the wheels glided on the blacktop underneath me, I made up
dramatic tales and told them to myself aloud. I can't imagine what
my neighbors must have thought of the spectacle—a young girl riding
around aimlessly, talking to herself. But I realize now that I was working on my own story, dreaming up exquisite characters and exhilarat-
ing experiences to will them into reality. From the seat of my bike, I

composed the melody of my life with the prodigal vision of a Mozart.

The more the world called my body too big and my being too much (and not enough), the more my orchestral symphony faded. Or maybe I stopped listening. The music that once moved me for hours was replaced by background noise, like radio static, the voices of other people becoming louder and louder and more relentless—until finally I couldn't hear my own music anymore, let alone remember what it used to sound like.

Instead of pursuing my passion for art, I went to law school and hated nearly every bit of it. The forty-minute drive from my parents' home to the Northern Illinois University College of Law during the first year of my legal studies typically included this internal refrain: *What the fuck have I done? How the hell did I get here?*

Everything in me had to resist the nagging impulse to turn my car around and drive off to anywhere other than where I was.

But I didn't turn the car around. The ever-dutiful and diligent unhappy achiever, I willed myself to stay the course. I'd worked hard to get into law school, after all, and my family was counting on me to finish. Besides, I knew my grandmother would be more excited to brag about her granddaughter "the lawyer" than her granddaughter "the writer."

Someone once told me that if you want to know your life's purpose, remember what you loved to do when you were eight. When we were eight, things we did for fun and play, we did for no reason other than happiness. We had no agenda, no goals to achieve, no boss on our backs. A society consumed with external trappings of wealth, domination, and success hadn't taken hold of our psyches enough yet to convince us that if we weren't doing something for a reason other than joy, it wasn't worth doing. Whatever we chose to do, we did with absolute abandon and pleasure.

Your calling doesn't have to be your day job. It doesn't have to earn you money. You don't have to be good at it. But that doesn't mean it isn't worth doing.

We leave our eight-year-old selves behind with no recollection of what that version of us looked like, let alone what they loved. Singing and dancing, playing and dreaming, like we did when we were kids, fills us up and helps us find our purpose. Our passion for living, believing, and loving things is bigger and more breathtaking and beautiful than all the boxes the world built for us to fill.

When we were children, we didn't question if we were worthy of doing something just because we enjoyed it. We sought out fun and play without having done anything of cultural merit or social significance. It's not about doing nothing. It's about being brave enough to be the thing you're most called to be, regardless of whether it pays the bills, evokes prestige and praise, or pleases your grandmother.

Imagine how much healing humankind could engender if we gave ourselves the grace to stop standing on the sidelines of our lives, listening to someone else's song—and instead, set our souls free to dance again.

CHAPTER 24

Masks & Mirrors

It is amazing how revealing our limitations can feel like discovering a magic wand of love, compassion, and understanding. Confronting our own ugliness grants us the gift of seeing others, even those with whom we've had difficult relationships, in a more beautiful light.

"You're using kindness to control people."

This declaration from my therapist threw me like I'd driven a car at ninety miles per hour into a median with no seat belt. The worst part was she'd just interrupted my devastating story of friendship betrayal to deliver it to me. Sure, I may have been spiraling into judgment, criticism, and self-pity. But I was a clear victim in all the bullshit I recounted in painstaking detail on her couch. How dare she use this moment to deprive me of this time to feel sorry for myself? I fucking paid for it, after all.

No one had told me I signed up for brutally uncomfortable candor, and I momentarily considered requesting a refund. I knew that the facts I needed to help me grow and heal wouldn't always be warm and fuzzy. But with one sentence, my therapist dismantled a picture of myself I had spent a lifetime painting: *I am kind. I am loving. I treat people with respect. I am gentle.*

The reality bearing down on me didn't match these descriptions. It sounded more like this: *I am controlling. I am inauthentic. I use kindness to manipulate. I use goodness to stay safe.*

These words didn't have the same ring as the ones I'd previously associated with me. I preferred mine, and I wanted to be outraged and aghast by the accusation my therapist leveled at me. I was kind. Very, very kind. And I worked hard to be kind. So what if my kindness wasn't always pure? The effects of my kindness were the same, even if the feelings behind it sometimes weren't. Anyway, it was only our second session. How could she determine my kindness was a facade in less than two hours? I'd been listening to my stories for thirty-eight years, and I'd never seen the truth in my lies.

In the moment in which I was revealed to myself, I felt embarrassed and exposed. Most of all, though, I was overcome by deep, penetrating shame. The kind that strikes without warning and starts seeping out of every pore like the steady drip of a leaky faucet.

Tense and red-faced, I listened as my therapist explained what she meant: "It's as if all of your interactions with the outside world are being filtered through a mask." She interlaced her fingers and raised her hands a foot in front of her, obscuring her eyes and face. "Trauma compelled you to create this mask as a means of safety and security," she said. "But it's also a way to control the world around us when we believe the only alternative to controlling people is to be controlled by them."

All this time I'd worn a mask to protect me from monsters, but it turned out that the monster looked a lot like me.

Admitting this left me shaken. I thought I'd already unearthed all the stories about myself that led me to succumb to being an unhappy achiever. But suddenly, my shrink exposed yet another of my self-serving narratives. Healing is like an onion, and as soon as one pungent layer is removed, another layer waits at the ready for its chance to turn our psychic tastebuds sour. She held up a mirror, and it wasn't the rose-colored kind I normally examined my reflection in. It was much clearer and more honest, revealing truths I wasn't expecting or prepared for. But it was time.

Somehow, pointing out my warts and imperfections gave me the pause I needed to see the humanity in my former friends. It didn't excuse the ways in which they'd betrayed my confidence or hurt my heart. But it enabled me to recognize that I wasn't blameless, either.

I could never be completely without fault because I am, in the words of my former high school history teacher, "an FHB." A fallible human being—and, apparently, one with serious control issues.

It is amazing how revealing our limitations can feel like discovering a magic wand of love, compassion, and understanding. Confronting our own ugliness grants us the gift of seeing others, even those we've had difficult relationships with, in a more beautiful light. Deconstructing images of ourselves we've clung to for decades is gutting. It's like walking around with your insides spilling out. All the exterior walls built to block pain start to crumble, and everything we took for granted about ourselves and others is reduced to rubble.

We're forced to acknowledge that people are too complicated and complex to distill down to either victim or villain. Yet, that's usually our go-to whenever we feel hurt or harmed by someone else. They're bad; I'm good. No situation involving human beings is ever that simple. If anything, we should say to ourselves: *They're afraid; I am, too.*

Fear brings out the worst in all of us. It leads us to say terrible things and behave in ways we never would have believed we were capable of. Sometimes, it compels us to commit acts against each other so egregious we can't even admit them to ourselves. That's when we need mirrors the most. When we're not capable of confronting our darkness, the best we can hope for is an empathetic ear to help us wade through it until we find the light. Eventually, all that fear is replaced by faith.

Faith that we're lovable without doing so much to seem good.

Faith that who we are, authentically, will always be enough.

Faith that being fallible is better than pretending to be perfect.

Then eventually, without realizing it, our masks fall away, and people start to see us for the first time.

CHAPTER 25

Love Her & Leave Her

A good ending doesn't always mean a happy ending.
But we can create new, better endings for ourselves and others
over time. Even when we face a devastating, earth-shattering
ending, one that is completely out of our control, we have the capacity
to reconnect with ourselves and our truth. We can transcend
the pain and expand wider into wholeness through healing.

Early on, I learned that the people I love most will leave. As a child, I developed abandonment issues when it came to friends. It took me a lifetime to recognize this and reckon with it. I couldn't figure out why I held on to friendships like life preservers, clinging to them for dear life as if letting go would mean drowning alone in open water. I did so despite every sign indicating that these relationships were long past their expiration dates. I did so even when my interactions with the people upon whom I'd once lovingly bestowed the label of "friend," treated me like anything but a friend, at least according to most definitions.

When considering the meaning of friendship, I always thought of a song we used to sing in my elementary school Girl Scout troop: "Make new friends, but keep the old. One is silver, and the other's gold." Naively, I believed every friend I loved would be a friend, by my side, forever.

It's one of the cultural lessons we're indoctrinated with early on. Especially when it comes to media representations of female friendship, the message that friends are loyal, lifelong companions couldn't be clearer: *Thelma and Louise*; CC and Hillary in *Beaches*; Mary Richards and Rhoda Morgenstern. These pairs were proof that girls were meant to have forever friendships. It wasn't the same for boys—outside of bonds of brotherhood formed in war dramas, portrayals of platonic relationships between men aren't typically accompanied by the same level of emotional intensity, commitment, longevity, or codependency. But for girls, friendships were as essential as air. I embarked upon life believing that every person I befriended would be with me until the bitter end.

This belief system made losing a friend feel like a failure. I viewed every failed friendship as an indictment: *What's wrong with me that she doesn't like me anymore? What did I do that caused her to treat me like this? Why doesn't she love me like I love her?*

As an unhappy achiever, always laser-focused on how everyone else felt while discounting and disregarding my own feelings, I couldn't conceptualize the possibility that perhaps the end of a relationship with a friend could be the best outcome for both of us and didn't necessarily mean anyone did anything wrong. It wasn't a reflection of some grave personal shortcoming or inadequacy. It just, well, *was*.

Endings happen. Sometimes they occur through conscious choice when we implement changes and integrate new belief patterns and behavioral practices into our lives. But sometimes, endings happen to us, such as when we lose someone before we believe we're ready to. It's all part of the inevitable flow of our existence. We can't have new beginnings without endings, and we can't create space to bring in new experiences to facilitate growth without some form of letting go.

Endings, especially painful ones, aren't necessarily a reflection of something we did or deserved. They aren't always earned, just as they aren't always unearned. They're unavoidable and as inexorable along our journey here as life is to death. Often, the best gift we can give ourselves and others is the best possible ending. After all, good endings are good for everyone.

A good ending doesn't always mean a happy ending. But we can create new, better endings for ourselves and others over time. Even when we face a devastating, earth-shattering ending, one that is completely out of our control, we have the capacity to reconnect with ourselves and our truth. We can transcend the pain and expand wider into wholeness through healing. Endings carve out paths to our desires. They chart courses for our lives we couldn't conceive of before. Sometimes, they're a slight course correct; sometimes, they're a superhighway to a destination we didn't see coming. Regardless, letting go of what no longer serves us can lead to our life's biggest blessings.

This is a lesson I'm still learning after nearly four decades on this planet, though my seven-year-old daughter seems to know it innately. Alex is the girl embodiment of the woman I want to be "when I grow up." She's secure in herself in a way I wasn't at her age. She has an aura and quiet confidence that let me know she already understands who she is and what she's here to do, even if the rest of us aren't aware of it yet. For her, childhood is a formality, something she's biding her time to get through as she waits for the big things she's destined to do here later.

One night, while we were sharing a family dinner, my nine-year-old son, Ari, announced, "Alex's friends were running away from her at recess today." Concerned, Aaron and I looked up from our plates of pasta in unison.

"What?" I asked. "Is that true, Alex?"

She looked over at her older brother with an expression signaling relief that she could share something that bothered her along with annoyance that he'd blurted it out without warning or permission.

"Yes," she said quietly.

"How did that make you feel, honey?" I asked, although we already knew the answer.

"S-A-D," she spelled aloud.

We talked through her encounter on the playground for the rest of dinner. Each of us took turns offering whatever we could muster to help her process her feelings and ease her hurting heart. A couple of days later, I checked in with her to see how things were going at school.

"Alex," I said, putting my arm around her, "how is everything with the friends who were running away from you?"

"Well," she began, her voice trailing off a bit before she continued, "one of them is trying to talk to me and pretend nothing happened. She said she wants me to come over to her house to play."

Awesome! I thought to myself. *Those girls are being kind to her now!*

Despite my relief and excitement, I played it cool: "Oh, nice. Do you want to go to her house for a playdate?"

"No, I don't think I do," she said.

I affirmed it was her choice, and I'd support whatever she decided. Inside, though, I was flabbergasted and stunned. My first-grade daughter was doing something I never had: She was prioritizing her feelings, her well-being, and her truth over another person's apology. She wasn't relying on others to determine what decision was right. She wasn't telling herself that because someone else humbled themselves enough to atone, they were entitled to her time. She was looking inside and making her own autonomous, heartfelt decision.

Alex's ending may only be temporary. She may later choose to let the friends who left her behind on the playground back into her circle. But I have no doubt that if my daughter does, it will be in her readiness, following the call of her own inner wisdom, rather than allowing the flights and fancies of other first-graders to decide her happiness, or lack thereof, for her.

We don't get to choose when someone we cherish or invest ourselves in leaves us behind or abandons us, whether on the school playground or the playground of life. But we can say goodbye with gratitude—honoring ourselves, our shared experiences, and the gifts they gave us before they were gone.

CHAPTER 26

Voice

I don't ingest other people's pain and projections anymore.
Everyone's entitled to his or her own opinions, interpretations,
and judgments, and so am I. I have a voice, and now, whether it's
in personal relationships with friends and family or with a staff
member at my son's school, I use it.

"You should have held the door open for me."

The Amazon deliveryman's words ripped me out of a trancelike stupor. I was standing inside the double doors of my son Ashton's preschool, consumed with anxious thoughts about an email I'd sent to the school secretary a couple hours earlier, when he walked by, muttering those words under his breath.

Was he talking to me? I wondered. I could have opened the door for him if I'd been paying attention. But I was spacing out, and my mind had been too preoccupied to process anyone or anything happening around me. The email dominating my thoughts was sent in response to a conversation I'd had with the preschool secretary at drop-off that morning.

"May I talk to you about something?" she'd asked.

These are words rarely followed by anything the person on the receiving end of the question wants to hear.

"Sure," I said, wishing I could decline her request.

"Yesterday, you were late picking Ashton up, and he kept asking me where his mommy was," she said, sounding as if I'd abandoned my boy at school instead of arriving ten minutes late to retrieve him. "He just gets so sad when you're not here at 12:30 p.m. like all the other parents."

All the other parents . . ., I thought. I wasn't like all the other parents at my son's preschool. She knew it, and I knew it. And my tardiness at pickup was the least obvious thing that separated me from them. They were Hasidic Jews, and I, although a descendant of Ashkenazi Jews, had never practiced the religion, so I was practically a *shiksa*. My bloodline might've been Jewish, but my appearance and lifestyle weren't.

I respected them and their ultraconservative, orthodox lifestyle. But my leather jackets and red lipstick made it clear I wasn't like them. The school secretary had been eyeballing me for months. She was mostly pleasant, but on the few occasions in which I'd arrived late to pickup, she practically ignored me.

"Hello," I'd say with a smile sent as a peace offering from me to her, hoping the sincerity in my face could bridge the gap between my being behind schedule and her annoyance. The only response she mustered in my direction was a sharp glare. Her icy-blue eyes matched her demeanor, piercing straight through me and sending me into a shame spiral. *Message received.*

So our conversation about my timeliness (or lack thereof) confirmed what I already knew: She was pissed and being passive aggressive about it. Whether it was the fact that she had to wait with my son until I arrived, or my shiksa ways, she was perturbed by me. And she let me know it, cloaking it not as an issue of prioritizing my personal responsibility for punctuality but by positioning it as an issue of my son's emotional well-being. She wanted me to believe that running ten minutes late to retrieve Ashton wasn't a problem for her, it was damaging to my child.

Seriously?

When I was growing up, my mother was the only mother in my parochial school class who worked outside the home. Both my parents had to work for our family's livelihood, and to afford tuition for the elementary education they felt was the best our small town could offer their daughter. I was routinely the last child waiting in the parking lot pickup line. There were times I was embarrassed by it, and every now and then,

I resented it. I wondered why my mother wasn't waiting, religiously, for me to burst out of the school's double doors at the end of every day with anticipation and a smile that signaled she'd been counting the hours until she took me home.

The answer, even if I didn't understand it then, was simple: she was fucking working.

Late was the best my mother could do while managing motherhood and a job. Managing, not balancing. Often, when we're trying to meet the demands of our unhappy-achieving, overscheduled lives, balance isn't just an illusion; it's an impossibility. My mother wasn't striving for balance. My mother was doing her best to survive.

And if her best was late, my adult self says that's okay, even if my eight-year-old self didn't understand. I've accumulated a bundle of emotional baggage to unpack with my therapist every other week, but one thing I'm not carrying around with me is my mother's lack of punctuality.

I don't know if it's inevitable to repeat some of the patterns of our parents. But I do know that although it's my responsibility to be on time, and I never want to leave my little guy waiting, like my mother, I'm doing my best. I don't always get it right. But I'll keep trying.

And when I fall short, I no longer see it as reflective of serious shortcomings or a lack of striving. I see it as a symptom of a soul engaged in a universal struggle to find her way, her stride, and her voice.

During the three and a half hours a day my son is at preschool, I cram as much writing work in as I can. Sometimes I try to do too much with too little time. I'm struggling to strike the right balance between a career that feeds my creative spirit and supports my family financially, since I am the primary caretaker for my three young children.

When my son's preschool secretary suggested my lateness could be hurting my child, I cried in the car on the way home that morning, comparing myself to all the other parents she cited, the ones who were always on time. In the past, I would have swallowed my shame and shut up. I would have let her tell the tale of my tardiness and internalized it, filing it away as another portrayal of imperfect me that must be true because someone else said it. But I'm no longer the lady who lets other people tell her who she is. I'm a grown-ass woman who defines herself, one who also sets her own boundaries and doesn't let bullshit stand as fact.

I don't ingest other people's pain and projections anymore. Everyone is entitled to his or her own opinions, interpretations, and judgments, and so am I. I have a voice, and now, whether it's in personal relationships with friends and family or with a staff member at my son's school, I use it.

Just like any other instrument I wasn't taught to play, I haven't mastered my voice yet, but I'm practicing my new skills. I can't say I was wrong to ask the school secretary to "confine conversations regarding logistical, scheduling, or administrative matters to the issues at hand." I also can't say I didn't err in the severity of my response to her. Nevertheless, I don't ignore my inner knowing in favor of the dictates of others. When that alarm bell in the depths of my body sounds, "Alert! Alert! Something's wrong!" I stop and listen. Then, I give it a voice.

I doubt the school secretary liked the tone of my message when it hit her email inbox, but at least it opened the door to a deeper dialogue between us. It led to a further exchange that included mutual apologies in a way that silence and stuffed-away hurts never would have. She may never like me as much as she likes all the other, more punctual parents at preschool, but that's not my business. It's my business to lead a more wholehearted, authentic, happy life.

And that's enough.

"Excuse me," I said to the Amazon deliveryman as he breezed by me on his way out of the school. "Did you say I should have held the door open for you?" He turned to look back at me, startled. I couldn't tell if he was surprised that I'd heard what he said or surprised that I asked. "No, actually, I was talking about him," he said, pointing toward another parent who had entered the building just before him.

"Oh, okay, thanks," I said. "Have a great day."

CHAPTER 27

Chameleons

I'd always been an energetic chameleon, changing colors to reflect everyone else. I could adapt my behavior, attitude, and opinions to comport with whoever happened to be sitting in front of me or on the other end of a phone line.

Being a chameleon came naturally before I was brave enough to reveal my true colors.

A friend and I had spent days exchanging texts and missing each other's calls, trying to find a time to catch up for a few minutes. In one of her messages, she told me there was a death in her family, so I knew she had a lot going on.

"How are you?" I asked, upon answering her call.

She sighed and took a breath before responding: "Not great. I made the mistake of volunteering to lead the annual art enrichment project at the kids' school, and my husband's grandmother, the beloved matriarch of his family, died this week." She went on to tell me that in addition to all the above, her youngest daughter, who suffers from pediatric kidney disease, relapsed.

That was a bad fucking week. We hadn't been friends for very long and were only beginning to get to know each other, but I felt awful for her and her family.

"I'm so sorry," I said, fumbling a bit as I figured out what to say. "Can I do anything to help lighten your load?"

I heard myself speaking, and I knew my response probably seemed prepackaged and trite. I knew she deserved better than that in return for her candor. I was a writer, for God's sake, a professional wordsmith. Yet suddenly, I couldn't find a single phrase that sounded suitable for this situation. But she didn't notice—she was more intent on changing the subject.

"Anyway, enough about that," she said. "How are you?"

It's incredible how a single, seemingly innocuous question can instantly change the course and content of a conversation. The spotlight was now shining on me, and the heat made me sweat.

Fuck . . . what do I say? I wondered.

The truth was that things in my world were fine. And not fine in the way we use it in polite conversation to deflect any discussion of how we're actually doing, especially when things are seriously shitty. My life was very much fine, so fine that at that moment it was almost nondescript. All that fine-ness made me worry I was a total bore. I had neither highs nor lows to share, a bit of a disappointment since the artist in me enjoys living with a healthy hint of drama.

Maybe it was okay, and even preferable, that I didn't have any sensational news to share. The last thing people going through hard times want to hear is that while their world is imploding, someone else is gifted with the secret to total world domination. This isn't to say I don't believe in the beauty of vicarious joy, sharing and taking pleasure in the good fortune and feelings of others. But I really didn't have anything exciting or celebratory to offer my new friend, and I had no idea if she even subscribed to the idea of sympathetic pleasure.

Once I ruled out positivity in my repertoire of socially desirable responses, I started sorting through the other obvious category: negativity.

Misery loves company, after all, right? *Think, Ash. Think.* I combed through my mind for one bad thing that had happened since we last spoke to each other. *Shit, there must be an example of recent bad luck filed away in my brain.*

Aha, there was! The week prior, we discovered the plumbing from our bathtub was connected to nothing after bathwater flooded our basement. This was a perfect slice of crap pie for us to enjoy together; the only problem was, I didn't think of it in time. Instead, after a few intense rounds of mental gymnastics, the most I could muster was: "Well, hmmm . . . you know, I guess everything over here's been—fine."

"Okay," she said. I sensed disappointment, or maybe boredom, so I followed up: "Yeah, I mean, everything's been pretty steady. I'm kinda just cruisin' along, I guess."

We hung up not long after that.

Afterward, I had legitimate questions about whether honesty was the right approach. The answer I gave my friend was the most genuine. In sharp contrast to all that was going on with her, nothing was really going on with me. But I was disappointed with myself for not making her feel like I was more in the suck with her.

Besides, I'd always been an energetic chameleon, changing colors to reflect everyone else. I could adapt my behavior, attitude, and opinions to comport with whoever happened to be sitting in front of me or on the other end of a phone line. It was a big part of how I performed "good." It seemed to make people the most happy and comfortable. And best of all, it kept me safe and relatively conflict-free.

Sadly, though, I accumulated people in my life who only interacted with me in that way, those who preferred me as a chameleon rather than a human being. When I stopped molding myself to match them, they decided "me" wasn't what they wanted. They said I'd changed. That I was no longer the person they once knew and "loved." But the truth was, they never saw the real me, let alone knew her.

Although it hurt to find out not everyone's love is unconditional, I couldn't fault them for it either.

I chose to be their chameleon instead of their friend. When I stopped hiding myself, being around me must've felt strange and unfamiliar. Suddenly, the shades and hues they saw in me were ones they didn't recognize. The person facing them wasn't as pleasing. She didn't give their feelings complete precedence over hers. Subtle passive aggression and disrespect she'd once swallowed without complaint suddenly wasn't as palatable. And she refused to deny her truth to protect them from pain or spare their fears.

I'm not a chameleon anymore. My sense of self has become too solid to come and go on the whims of people who enter and exit my life. Not everyone's going to like and accept who I am, but I refuse to dim or dull my light to fit in. I won't contort or control myself to the point of being fake for the sake of someone else's comfort. An honest state of being may not always seem as easy and smooth as my formerly reptilian existence. But the truth is that something I thought kept me safe was nothing but a surefire recipe for forming insecure, unstable attachments. The answer I gave my friend on the phone wasn't perfect; I wasn't able to commiserate in quite the way I wanted to. Still, I could listen with compassion and hold space for her experience.

The more I traded unhappy achieving for authenticity, the more rewarding and solid my relationships became. Being me may not always be who everyone wants me to be—but at least I attract people who embrace my true colors.

CHAPTER 28

Daydream Believer

No matter how resolute I am, the paths I pursue aren't always met with unwavering support from friends and family. Sometimes, they're met with sideways glances and skepticism. I don't care. Not caring has rendered me adept at daring to try—and daring to dream.

I've always had a hard time paying attention. Because I was a pleasing, perfectionist kind of kid, my parents were never summoned to the principal's office or received unfavorable reports about my behavior. This isn't to say I never got into trouble or did anything wrong. But a stringent desire to be good generally kept me from committing offenses grave enough to warrant parental notification or intervention.

Although my goodness shielded me from disciplinary issues, it didn't safeguard me against academic critique. Every year, my mother emerged from parent-teacher conferences with the same complaint from teachers: "Ashley's a good student, but she's a daydreamer." My butt might have been firmly planted in my desk chair, but my head was off in a more interesting place. My imagination sent me soaring through hours of solitary storytelling wherever I was—at home, riding my bike, and in school. It never ceased spinning tales of times and places I preferred to where I actually was.

Although it was a bit of an educational liability, dreaming is one of my superpowers. It enables me to picture possibilities that I can subsequently imagine into existence. I'm not talking about wonky *The*

Secret-type crap—I don't wait passively for "universal magic" to unfold and grant me my wishes. Instead, I see what I want, I begin to believe in the potential of making it happen, and I take meaningful steps to pursue it.

Most of the time, I have no fucking idea what I'm doing when I set out to make my dreams reality. And I've made more mistakes than I can count, many of which were painful and embarrassing. Even when it hurts, I keep moving. I keep trying. I understand that if I can perceive the end in my mind, I've already declared war against whatever resistance stands between me and achieving it. I allow myself to be pulled toward the path that's presented itself, and let the inertia transform me into a relentless force for the vision conjured somewhere in my subconscious.

No matter how resolute I am, the paths I pursue aren't always met with unwavering support from friends and family. Sometimes, they're met with sideways glances and skepticism. I don't care. Not caring has rendered me adept at daring to try—and daring to dream. Giving no fucks about whether everyone believes in the recipes I concoct for myself is a learned skill. It runs completely counter to the lot of unhappy achievers, individuals who typically invest too much stock in other people's approval. I gave far too many fucks for far too long. Dreaming was as second nature as breathing, but blocking out bullshit that might derail me from the way I wanted to go was a lot less innate.

Without the ability to put on healthy blinders when it comes to outside opinions that might derail us from our dreams, we're drivers using faulty GPS. We might know exactly where we need to go. We might even know the fastest, most efficient route to getting there. But instead of following our own internal compass, we take every senseless detour that pops up on our radar just because someone or something else suggested it.

I spent most of my years well versed in the self-sabotaging practice of second-guessing myself. My earliest memory of this occurred while traveling with my parents. We were on an airplane, and I was passing the time by drawing pictures. Looking for creative inspiration, I decided to draw a picture of what I wanted to be when I grew up, and I carefully crafted an image of me holding a paintbrush and wearing a beret.

When I finished, with a last stroke of color from my crayon, I presented it to my mother with pride. "Mom, I'm going to be an artist!" I declared, brandishing the custom portrait of my future in her direction.

She looked up from her magazine. "You're going to college. Why not be a doctor or a lawyer?" she asked.

Feeling deflated, I turned my sketch over on my tray table and silently wondered: *But what if I don't want to be a doctor or lawyer?*

Two decades later, I passed the Illinois State Bar exam. I can't condemn my mother for wanting what she believed was best for me, and although I've questioned whether working so hard to become an attorney was a waste of time, energy, and money, I don't regret it. It earned me a perpetual membership in an honorary, elite (albeit somewhat stodgy) professional club and gave me serious intellectual "street cred." It also constitutes a solid backup plan should an unexpected change in financial circumstances ever require me to dust off my trusty law license and trade my warm, fuzzy writing socks for boring blue blazers.

The adult version of me may have earned a Juris Doctor, but I was born to be an artist.

I don't wear a beret or paint with brushes like the artist depicted in my airplane masterpiece. Instead, I compose lyrical lines of text and create scenes from tapestries of words woven together with precision and intention. I'm not sure if it's ever dawned on my mother that despite a few detours, I grew up to be an artist, after all.

When I practiced law, I was assigned a windowless office, not much larger than a cubicle. It was completely bare, but for a metal desk and chair, a computer, and stacks upon stacks of files. I never hung a single item on its stark, inauspicious white walls, nor did I even attempt to soften the harshness of its fluorescent lighting by adorning it with sentimental trinkets or decor of any kind. The only indication anyone regularly inhabited the space was the occasional sighting of me sitting in there, or my black leather briefcase abandoned on the floor when I went to the restroom. The room was designated for me, but it didn't belong to me—or maybe I understood I didn't belong in it.

Last year, I set up a new office for myself. It's the first space I've designed for me, one uniquely mine and filled with things that make my soul sing. My workspace includes an inspirational wall of images of people whose footsteps I want to follow, and quotes of wisdom I hope to embody. Hanging above everything, serving as a literal and figurative theme for everything beneath it, is a sign that reads: "Daydream Believer."

When I saw the sign, I knew I had to have it. I'm pretty sure I've been a daydream believer since birth, and my inspiration wall provides the perfect physical representation of this part of myself. From mementos of pride-filled professional accomplishments to poems, it's all one big, eye-catching manifestation of the version of me I'm committed to being and the kind of world I'm dedicated to building. It illustrates the notion that if we visualize what's possible in rooms of our own, the energy we generate won't just be confined to four walls—it will be transcendent. What we look upon most can be abiding reminders of our values and the benchmarks we measure our behavior and decision-making against.

But for all the good that daydream believing can bring, as I mentioned earlier, it's not without pitfalls. Recently, a trusted mentor told me: "You struggle to be present." His words sliced through my core. I recognized this sensation as the feeling I get when I've been served a hearty helping of truth pudding. It's a gift, yet one as welcome as a fruitcake. He was right. At various points, I've struggled to resign myself to the moment I was in. Daydreaming about what could be is so much sexier than finding contentment with what already is. It is a reliable escape, a means to avoid anything tedious, undesirable, or confining. The problem is that even if we realize every one of our heart's desires, our lives will never be devoid of activities we'd prefer to avoid. These are the responsibilities that constantly require us to prioritize obligations over our inclinations or aspirations.

I once heard someone interviewed on NPR who declared he never does anything he doesn't want to do. When pressed about how this was possible, he argued that when it comes to doing chores like laundry, he *does* want to do them because he wants clean clothes. This made his argument sound like rhetorical fluff. Saying "I want clean clothes, so I want to do laundry" is like saying "I ate bad cheese and my stomach is churning, so I want to vomit." No one actually *wants* to throw up, but we are willing to kneel at the foot of the porcelain throne for a while if that's what it takes to feel better. And when I have to do laundry—or puke—it's pretty hard not to dream of being elsewhere.

Recently, though, I read a more convincing perspective on this issue. In the book *Think Like a Monk*, Jay Shetty writes about his time as a monk in a Hindu ashram, when he was routinely tasked with doing work he didn't want to do—menial, mind-numbing jobs like mopping floors and planting potatoes. However, over time, he found meaning in the mundane. For instance, cleaning floors might offer a lesson in precision or attention to detail, and planting potatoes could be a reminder of our connection to the earth or a literal reminder that growth can require us to get down in the dirt.

I'm learning to adopt these principles in my daily life to ensure that my daydream-believing soul doesn't distract me from the abundance of my present life. This helps to bring the imaginative into the real world with me: After all, the challenge of a nonfiction writer is to translate ordinary experiences into words that make their ordinariness seem extraordinary while still being true. "I took out the garbage" isn't as vivid and interesting as "I lugged the cold, cumbersome plastic can behind me, writhing against the stench of a week's worth of waste."

I stay anchored in the real world as much as I can because I want my children to experience me as a mother whose presence is palpable and whose undivided attention affirms her love for them—not one whose body is near while the rest of her is not.

I believe we're all born daydream believers, whether or not we have signs hanging in our offices that say so. But it's a fine line between a healthy habit of paying attention to all of life's possibilities and a disengaged disregard for the preciousness of the present moment. The sweet spot is where our ability to believe in new beginnings and a brighter future makes the reality of our everyday lives more magical.

And, hopefully, a little dreamier.

CHAPTER 29

But I'm Awesome

\ı/

The shadows most of us see in ourselves when we look in the mirror
rarely surprise us. We may not want to stare at them for too long, or
we may pretend we don't see the darker hues in our own reflection.
But we can decide that our shadow selves aren't signs or symptoms of
unworthiness or ugliness, but evidence of being gloriously human.

Aaron swears his secret to self-love is one soul-affirming mantra:
"But I'm awesome."

This isn't just something he says to himself to dampen or diminish deep-seated insecurities. He believes it, in earnest. And Aaron isn't arrogant. He doesn't see himself as flawless or faultless. He understands his strengths and is at peace with his weaknesses. He admits his mistakes. He knows he messes up, and sometimes he says or does things he shouldn't, which might hurt others. When he does, he apologizes and tries his best to make amends. And after his missteps have been atoned for, he reminds himself: "Yeah, I fucked up. But I'm still awesome."

His unwavering understanding of his own awesomeness isn't shaken by his flaws or faults. It doesn't depend on how he's treated or perceived by others. All of that exists on the periphery, but awesomeness is the core center from which his confidence springs. And that is a beautiful, awe-inspiring way of being for a recovering unhappy achiever like me to behold.

It's also super fucking annoying. As someone who typically takes too much responsibility for other people's stuff and employs a stringent practice of self-flogging whenever I fall short of anyone's expectations (especially my own), Aaron's steadfast self-love can be somewhat irritating. And what's the natural next step when something about someone else highlights a shortcoming in ourselves?

Attack.

We get to work poking holes in their wholeness. I might think, *Who does Aaron think he is championing himself? Why doesn't he serve himself the same unhealthy, heaping dose of self-hatred I dish out to myself? And where the hell is his false modesty? He has a lot of nerve, liking himself so much!*

In the past, when Aaron would state his abiding love for himself without equivocation, I'd try to point out any part of him I deemed a work in progress. "Well, yeah, you're sure of yourself, but don't you think you can be emotionally unavailable?" I'd ask, as if I needed to prove my case that he needed fixing as much as I did.

Again, though, I missed the mark. Drawing attention to Aaron's alleged deficiencies was as futile as it was unkind. To his credit, Aaron never proclaimed to be perfect. He merely accepted himself, all of him, without exception. So, it didn't matter what unflattering facts I found in my arsenal. No truth bullet I hurled his way could penetrate its target. Aaron doesn't bother debating aspects of himself that could be better because they're beside the point. He chooses to believe he's awesome anyway.

Now, before you suggest that Aaron's self-image isn't particularly impressive because he's merely carrying himself with the confidence reserved for white men in America, I'll acknowledge that being white and male in our culture often accompanies privileges and positive presumptions. And these certainly can provide someone with a more solid foundation for building a stronger sense of self than most. Still, attributing all of Aaron's belief in his awesomeness to demographics oversimplifies and disregards his lived experiences and personal journey.

Aaron isn't a product of inherited affluence. For the first half of his childhood, he was raised by a single mother who relied on social programs and sewed her son's clothes in order to survive financially. Not having enough money was a source of worry and shame for Aaron as a kid. He got a paper route as soon as he was old enough and has worked ever since. He paid for college through military service that sent him into two wars and twenty-seven months of deployments. He did this to build a firm financial future for himself and his family, and to ensure that money was never worrisome again.

Aaron describes himself as a "nerdy, gangly kid" who learned how to be "cool." He wasn't terribly coordinated, so he couldn't rely on athletic prowess to ascend the teenage social stratosphere. To become more popular, he used his wit and sense of humor to fit in and find dates. Caring teachers, who believed in him, taught Aaron to highlight his strengths instead of getting bogged down by his blemishes. Harnessing the power of his gifts early on helped him to overcome later limitations with ease.

Aaron doesn't delude himself about who he is. He doesn't need his wife to hold his warts under a microscope so he can dissect them. But he also refuses to allow his imperfections to detract from his beauty. He believes that every aspect in the portrait of himself has been painted by his own colorful blend of life experiences. And so, he loves it all.

The shadows most of us see in ourselves when we look in the mirror rarely surprise us. We may not want to stare at them for too long, or we may pretend we don't see the darker hues in our own reflection. But we can decide that our shadow selves aren't signs or symptoms of unworthiness or ugliness, but evidence of being gloriously human.

I can't say I've fully integrated into my own psyche the sort of self-love Aaron embodies. Undoing the decades of conditioning that made me adept in the art of self-shaming, a socially acceptable form of self-harm (particularly for women), isn't easy. Cutting myself down with my own poison-dipped daggers may be as routine as brushing my teeth. But it also makes me feel like shit and leaves me more likely to slice through others with the same sharp edges of judgment and disdain I deliver myself daily. When we love and accept our shadow sides, we increase our capacity to love and accept the same in others. Despite serious marital struggles, Aaron has always embraced my obnoxious quirks and idiosyncrasies, deeming endearing what others would find enraging. Because the compassionate, unconditional love he applies to himself, he affords to the rest of us, too.

I can be moody. Sometimes I'm an intoxicating cocktail of passion and inspiration; at others, I'm a bitter, acidic sip of vinegar. I can be harsh, sharp-tongued, and quick to anger. I can be impatient, expecting answers and results with an entitled urgency. I can overtalk, taking too many words to say too many things no one needs to know. I can take up too much space—a formerly shy, unseen girl who needs other people to see her sparkle to feel noticed. I can struggle to be present, preferring to live in my own mind instead of inhabiting my life. I am all these unflattering things and, I'm sure, many more.

But I'm awesome.

CHAPTER 30

Dylan

Maybe if we allowed ourselves to be who we wanted to be, we could stop destroying others for disappointing us. Maybe if we sing the songs of our own souls rather than expecting others to sing them for us, we'd be freer to live authentically.

I'm in love with Bob Dylan, although he doesn't know it. Celebrity infatuations are fun because they rescue us from the monotony of reality. We create a mythical connection between ourselves and some fantastical public figure, a bond that endures beautifully and blissfully in the safe inner sanctuaries of our psyches.

In my ridiculous, make-believe relationship with Bob Dylan, for example, we spend Saturday nights writing songs. Naturally, he devises the melodies, and I chime in with occasional word suggestions to supplement his verses. I refer to him as Robert because ours is a May-December romance, and in my mind the formality of "Robert" embodies the wisdom and esteem he's earned with age. Plus, he finds it endearing when I call him by his given name.

We may be an unlikely pair; indeed, we aren't a pair at all. But Bob Dylan is the perfectly imperfect partner for an unhappy achiever in recovery like me.

When I stumbled upon Martin Scorsese's Dylan documentary *No Direction Home* on Netflix, I had no expectations other than satisfying a deep interest in creativity and art. Of course, I'd heard Bob Dylan's music—even an "elder millennial" like me knows of the '60s icon. It's not hard to see why when contemplating timeless, poetic tunes like "The Times They Are A-Changin'."

But breathtaking lyrics aside, I fell madly in love with Bob for one simple reason: Bob Dylan doesn't give a fuck.

Although he's an unequivocal music legend, I'm less taken with his art than by who he is as an artist. Vintage film clips of Dylan getting booed on stage and called "Judas," chastised for evolving from straight folk to a blues-rock sound on ballads such as *Like a Rolling Stone*, were cringe-inducing. The more his fame and acclaim soared, the more fans and the media sought to box him in. They incessantly attempted to label him the holy father of folk and protest songs. They interrogated him to uncover the secrets of his popularity and resonance.

To their chagrin—and sometimes blatant outrage—Bob Dylan wouldn't satiate their appetites with the sorts of safe, palatable responses they craved. Many of his answers were satirical, even non-sensical. Dylan wasn't a social-justice or antiwar movement messiah; he was an ordinary man making music. So he spurned efforts to idealize him or reduce him to a cultural caricature.

We can't help but put famous people on pedestals. We love to sanctify them before we crucify them. We confuse their station in life for an implied promise to be who we want them to be, and then condemn them for breaking it. We can't accept them as mere mortals because we're convinced their money, talent, and position surpass their human-ness. But the unglamorous truth is this: "Celebrities, they're just like us."

Although the severity and level of scrutiny may differ, this type of behavior isn't reserved only for the most well known. We routinely subject ourselves and others to it. Punishment, in the form of social sanctions, is levied against people whenever they fail to fit our made-up molds, as if they're Jell-O instead of flesh and bone.

It's an insidious game we play. We expect people to behave in the most comfortable ways for us, acting in accordance with not only our beliefs and values but also, especially, our fears. When those around us fail to fit inside the narrow, suffocating boxes we construct to keep our-selves safe, we lash out, withdraw, gossip, judge, or criticize.

We feign outrage and contempt at "traitors," anyone who has the audacity to disregard our delicate sensibilities to save their own lives. We shout "Judas!" at their concerts or whisper behind their backs. Such are the consequences for failing to be the heroes we wanted them to be—so we wouldn't have to do the work of being our own heroes.

Maybe if we allowed ourselves to be who we wanted to be, we could stop destroying others for disappointing us. Maybe if we sing the songs of our own souls rather than expecting others to sing them for us, we'd be freer to live authentically.

I'm not Bob Dylan. Yet even for painfully ordinary folks like me, the price of changing from fictitious and constructed to organic and real can be high. Some will make you out to be the Judas of their stories when you're no longer content being an underdeveloped character in their chosen narratives. And I guess that's their prerogative.

If inadvertently exposing and triggering other people's fears and fallacies are the inconvenient consequences of living my truth, I don't mind. I'll be their sacrificial *traitor* a thousand times before I ever betray myself. I'll live (and die) on the razor-sharp edge of realness, risking comfort and safety for radical integrity. Because although my relationship with Bob Dylan is made up, the sincerity he inspires inside of me isn't. It's the fire that compels me to stop giving so many fucks, and the strength to put sensitive parts of my story on printed pages in service of something much bigger than myself.

CHAPTER 31

Hobbies & Have To's

Maybe part of the reason we end up as unhappy achievers is
because we constantly compel ourselves to do the stuff we think we
should do instead of doing what we want to do. "Shoulds" are the leaky
faucets of soul-affirming self-love. They create a steady drip of
unhappiness that drains our spirit.

Most of us don't allow ourselves the glorious gift of a hobby. Learning how to play guitar is one of the first hobbies I've had as an adult, and I waited until I was almost forty years old to attempt it. I'd wanted to give it a go for most of my life, but I couldn't justify regularly undertaking an activity that wasn't "for something."

In other words, making time in my routine for the sole purpose of pleasure seemed senseless. I told myself nothing was worth doing unless its effect was greater than personal joy. As a woman with grown-ass responsibilities and demands, how could I rationalize diverting my resources and attention to a purposeless pastime?

Here is the answer: I don't rationalize. I just allow myself to engage with pleasure.

Nowadays, being myself takes precedence, and being myself includes doing all the cool shit I dreamed of but never made it a priority to try. And most of the time, it involves me doing those things badly. Like, seriously, badly.

Last winter, I set out to become a snowboarder. I'm not proficient in any winter sport, and snowboarding looked like the sexiest of the lot. It turns out it might be the most difficult and dangerous, too. I spent most of January, February, and March getting chewed up and spit out by every unfortunate mountain I confronted. I never "shredded" a single one; instead, they shredded the fuck out of me. Still, no matter how bruised my poor tailbone was, or how much snow I ate, I refused to accept defeat.

Until, of course, I was midway down a relatively easy—albeit icy—slope, practicing toe-side turns, when I crashed headfirst into unforgiving ground. I don't recall much beyond that, except that I got up, brushed myself off, and finished the run. I'm sure of this because Aaron, unaware of the calamity that had just taken place, snapped a picture of me sailing through the snow with my ski goggles dangling from the back of my helmet. I didn't know it yet, but I was cruising along with a concussion. Apparently, one becomes a bit discombobulated after a head injury.

Aaron realized I'd sustained some sort of neurological trauma when he greeted me at the foot of the hill and our conversation resembled a scene from the film *50 First Dates*, a romantic comedy in which the main character dates a woman suffering from short-term memory loss. I kept repeating myself and asking questions I should have known the answers to. Someone can only declare, "Honey, I think I got my bell rung!" with the same enthusiasm and voice inflection so many times before their "honey" rushes them to the emergency room.

I may never snowboard again. Knocking my noggin so hard I temporarily lost my faculties, which my passion, art, and profession depend on, may have scared me off the mountains for good. If I succumb to this newly formed, and perhaps well-justified, fear of surfing in snow, at least I can say I tried. The mountains of every ski destination might be a little more peaceful without me; and my fellow winter-sports enthusiasts, who otherwise would have had the unfortunate luck of coming into nonconsensual contact with me and my unwieldy board, might be a bit safer as well.

A great thing about hobbies is that the stakes are high if you don't try, and the stakes are low if you do. If you don't try, you may never know what talents and joys you might bring into your life; and if you do try, you can always stop if your engagement isn't bringing you happiness. Because I accepted the call to become a totally rad, gnarly snowboarder, I can now feel comfortable and confident tapping out.

Guitar, on the other hand, has stuck with me. It's not an extreme sport, and I may never get good enough to "shred" the fretboard. But unlike traversing Mother Nature's most treacherous, ice-covered inclines with both feet strapped to a medievally torturous board, it probably won't result in life-altering injuries. (Hearing loss may be a real risk, given my tendency to jam out to excessively loud music. Fortunately, modern hearing aids seem quite effective should the need arise.)

Although it hasn't been nearly as risky or painful as snowboarding, committing to guitar as a hobby hasn't been all fancy-free fun and unbridled passion, either. Many days, I drag myself to my instrument with the same lack of enthusiasm typically reserved for dragging myself to the gym at dawn. But I want to become a reasonably proficient amateur musician, just as I want to remain a reasonably fit person. Even if practicing sometimes feels as tedious as a blurry-eyed morning workout.

Learning anything requires regular effort, energy, and motivation. Whenever I'm running low on all the above, I mull over a million reasons why I should quit:

I don't need this extra stress, I might brood. *Guitar is just one more thing I have to remember to do.* Despite dancing one step away from musical defeat, I stubbornly persist. I reject the serpentlike temptation to succumb to the crotchety, old voice of my ego, one that says there's no value in leisure for its own sake.

Besides, my heart holds a deeper truth about my chosen hobby.

On rare occasions when I create enough space in my schedule to stand barefoot with my black-and-white Les Paul affixed to my shoulder, strumming away at whatever song strikes me—from rock classics like Zeppelin's "Black Dog" and AC/DC's "Back in Black" to "MMMBop," courtesy of the blond '90s pop trio Hanson—I'm flying high.

I'm liberated by the act of being true to myself in one of the most authentic ways possible. Uninhibited creative expression is a small respite from the mind-numbing matrix of modern existence. It's a subtle act of rebellion and resistance in which we own our right to do something simply because it speaks to us. Doing something for delight or to fulfill a dream isn't for nothing. It isn't frivolous. It's for *you,* and *you* deserve it.

As someone constantly at risk of forgetting my funny and taking myself too seriously, strumming my guitar is the closest I can come to childlike play and wonder. Sincere, unadulterated fun, in any form, nourishes us from the inside out, especially when it challenges the often-held belief that we must move through life like we're walking in mud. Lumbering, slogging, and slaving until we die. And that anything we do should be in service to the "success system."

The success system refers to the social order and supporting principles that allegedly guarantee a "good life." It teaches us that happiness hinges on obtaining impressive material things and achieving major milestones. It tells us to seek inner fulfillment with a singular focus on fulfilling external expectations. It sets us on a quest to do the things the world says we should, while losing sight of what we actually want.

Maybe part of the reason we end up as unhappy achievers is because we constantly compel ourselves to do the stuff we think we *should* do, instead of doing the things we *want* to do.

"Shoulds" are the leaky faucets of soul-affirming self-love. They create a steady drip of unhappiness that drains our spirit. Shoulds are too often confused with "have to's." Have to's are nonnegotiable necessities for survival. They're universal and unavoidable. However, if we carefully look at our perpetual list of have to's, I wonder how many of them we'd identify as shoulds in disguise.

Hobbies are a hall pass out of the eternal, self-imposed hell of shoulds. They reinforce our inner plumbing, so we can flow out into the world with vigor and abundance we wouldn't have otherwise. They get us used to doing activities just because they bring us joy, so we can engage in life joyfully, rather than out of obligation.

More than this, though, hobbies inspire wily, unlikely adventures, lead us down least-traveled roads, and expose us to fantastic and fascinating folks.

Like Bob Dylan.

Some may think playing mediocre guitar at midlife is a colossal waste of energy and a complete time suck. Maybe for them it would be. All I know is that four to five days a week, it's the closest I'll ever come to being onstage with my true love, Bob Dylan. And that's worth it.

CHAPTER 32

Princesses & Witches

We thought if we solved life's equation right, one day we'd skip
through a meadow with bluebirds singing. Instead, when we arrive
at the place where the meadow was promised to be, we realize it's
nothing but a picturesque prison. It has all the elements of an epic
tale, but it's a meaningless myth. Still, there we are, adorned in all
the trappings of proper princesses, wondering if being witches would
have been a lot more fun.

The closer I come to midlife, the more I sense a restlessness within me and the women in my circle.

More and more, the casual conversations between us over a cup of coffee or glass of wine center on one uncomfortable theme: our collective confinement.

We've checked off most of the boxes on our laundry lists of lifetime achievements, at least according to the definitions ingrained in us by the contemporary "cult of true womanhood" and the lives of princesses depicted in the Disney movies we grew up with. We made ourselves "attractive" and married "good" men. We made ourselves "smart" by buying expensive degrees. We made ourselves "independent" by building careers. And we put parts of ourselves on the back burner while we bore children.

We believe we did all of this of our own accord, with deliberate acts of will in a country that convinced us we were nothing but free. So why the fuck do we feel so trapped? Stuck? Bamboozled?

Recently, a friend said to me, "I have the husband, the baby, the big house in the 'burbs, and the job I broke my back for. Yet all I do is hustle to keep my life afloat, worrying and working to maintain this lifestyle. The weight of that responsibility can be crushing. And the irony is, when I was single and making half as much money, paying $450 a month in rent and squandering the rest of my salary on traveling and shoes, I felt so much more alive."

We're not merely constrained by chains of domesticity; we're smothered by the weight of supporting and nourishing everyone except ourselves.

Taught that being good women means tending to needs that aren't ours, many of us wouldn't know a healthy boundary if it bit us on the back of the neck. "Yes" is our automatic answer whenever a request is made of us. It's been said, though, that every yes is an IOU to be paid in full later in the precious currency of time. Although these debts are easily incurred, they're not so easily paid, and they add up fast.

Perhaps our propensity to enslave ourselves in service of the external wouldn't be so detrimental if we also said yes to ourselves more often. However, we're remarkably adept at saying no to ourselves. Most of the time, we don't even have to go to the trouble of turning ourselves down because we never thought to ask ourselves for gifts or grace in the first place.

How can we prioritize someone we're conditioned to forget? Who we were before we belonged to everyone else escapes our memory. Then, at some point in our pursuit of a Disney-princess fairy tale, our own story becomes overwritten. So, it isn't hard to understand why we eventually feel caught within the confines of our own creation. After all, unlived lives don't equate to happy ones, and no amount of contrived goodness can make us whole.

Inauthentic selves defined by the whims and wishes of others will never turn into anything solid. Even seemingly well-built houses grounded in genuine love and family bonds can feel as crumbling and cold as empty castles when we discover the tales we thought held the magic formula of a fulfilling life are as fake and phony as the two-dimensional characters they depicted.

We thought if we solved life's equation right, one day we'd skip through a meadow with bluebirds singing. Instead, when we arrive at the place where the meadow was promised to be, we realize it's nothing but a picturesque prison. It has all the elements of an epic tale, but it's a meaningless myth. Still, there we are, adorned in all the trappings of proper princesses, wondering if being witches would have been a lot more fun.

Fortunately, it's never too late to put aside our false tiaras and get witchy.

I'm not referring to the trope of the mean, evil, warty woman with a pointy black hat and broom, the one intended to scare us into passive submission with frightening tales of what will happen to us if we aren't good. Here, I'm calling for a reclamation and reincarnation of the witchy women who were historically castigated, shamed, and murdered merely for being themselves.

I'm talking about women who believed their femininity was as divine as masculinity. Who understood love as the one real source of human power; and who identified feminine values of empathy, compassion, sensitivity, and tenderness as sacred and healing.

They were magical in their courage to transcend the rules that devalued feminine existence through radical connection to and reliance on inner authority and authenticity. They were bearers of truth—not "golden rules" but potent inner wisdom.

It may seem odd that listening to and designating oneself the sole expert in one's own life would be revolutionary or witchy. But for many women, particularly those of the unhappy achieving variety, it is. We're taught to not trust ourselves, so we please and serve others. It might even be one of the primary causes of our continued disempowerment.

Perhaps the reason self-assured women tend to be designated witches is because they're the hardest to enslave. They're the least likely to surrender the birthright of their intrinsic being and worthiness in service of a system designed to subjugate them.

Fortunately, we no longer have to worry about literal burnings at the stake as a consequence of nonconformity. I can't promise, though, that dabbling in "the craft" won't lead to witch hunts and executions of a more figurative variety. Society tends to penalize women who have the audacity and conviction to please themselves first.

Such attacks are often most acute from women who struggle with other women's power, especially when it's subversive. When a woman is rendered insecure by the transformative potential of another woman, she's apt to use judgmental gossip to turn a happy witch back into an unhappy princess.

Becoming a real witch requires tenacity, commitment to healing, confidence to let others glow, and above all, a shitload of spunk. This level of chutzpah is innate. It isn't something we need to acquire; it's something we need to unbury from somewhere inside our bellies.

The aspects of us we hid when others said they were hideous are usually some of our most beautiful attributes. So let your snakes out of their cages and blow the fucking dust off the most faded facets of who you are. Poof.

I *am* a witch.

Witch is a label sexist, misogynistic cultures have employed to execute the majority of their victims for being female. I call myself a witch to reclaim a term used to torture and kill countless innocent people, mostly women. Many of these so-called witches weren't witches at all, according to any definition or law, nor did they identify themselves as such. I honor the memory of those for whom the designation of *witch* became a death sentence, and I remind myself that embracing my witchiness without fear is a blessing.

Being witchy is about being our best, brazen, badass selves. It is about prioritizing important aspects of who we are without apology, even when doing so undermines our society's princess ideals and people condemn us.

For me, this has come to mean everything from making sense of my life by transcribing it into raw, honest accounts for people to read to using credit card points to fly solo to Phoenix to attend a Bob Dylan concert. One woman might get a tattoo she's always wanted, while another with an admiration for Indigenous American tribes might embark on a pilgrimage to a reservation.

It doesn't matter what we do, as long as our *doing* reflects our truth. This is the set of keys to release us from the suffocating confinement of a princess's tower. This is the door to eternal liberation that social, cultural, and political forces seeking to sustain the status quo of feminine existence would rather stay locked. But once we've acquired the keys and amassed the courage to reenter the room where our essence resides, the only question that remains is:

Are we brave enough to be witches?

CHAPTER 33

Bees

*After so many stings, it can be nearly impossible to remember who
we were before life pierced us the first time. It might not be realistic to
believe that we can return to the pureness of perspective we possessed
before we realized that some bees would wound us. Still, I can't help
but think there's significance for that solitary little girl swimming
in the buggy pool.*

My earliest childhood memory involves bees.
I was four years old, wading in a plastic kiddie pool in the backyard. Although the cool tub of water delighted me, the grass and bugs
floating on the surface suggested the water wasn't particularly fresh.
So, I cupped my hands to fish out debris.

My method worked well for a minute or two, until I reached for the
wrong insect. Too young to associate the black-and-yellow-striped,
furry creature in front of me with anything unpleasant, I let the water
beneath it wash through my fingers as the bug settled against my skin.
Suddenly, the seemingly innocuous critter sent me spiraling from
dreamlike reverie into pulsating pain.

Before the sting, the sight of bees inspired carefree curiosity. Afterward, their presence meant imminent danger. It's remarkable how
innocence and intrigue give way to terror and dread in an instant.

My son's first encounter with stinging insects was very different. Ari
feared them long before he ever felt their sting. Aaron and I did our
best to alleviate our son's terror over the potential agony that awaited

him if his worst fear manifested. We felt his fear was far more fantastical than well founded, so without completely discounting his worries, we worked together to reassure him that he'd be fine as long as he left the fright-inducing bugs alone.

Nevertheless, when Ari was five years old, his fear went from nightmare to waking reality. A hot summer afternoon spent playing in the backyard spiraled from peaceful to panicked in a matter of seconds when a hornet got stuck underneath his shirt. Unable to escape the cotton prison of Ari's clothing, the scared insect stung his chest several times.

Not only did my son get stung, he got stung repeatedly—and traumatically. And it took time before Ari felt safe going outside again. His backyard had become a hazardous jungle instead of a familiar safe haven. It also undermined our subsequent efforts to convince my son that fear for its own sake is futile. His experience proved his fears weren't unfounded.

Ari's point of view prior to his first sting might have been different from mine—his solid sense of aversion and self-preservation versus my naive innocence and optimism. But, in the end, neither perspective spared us from getting stung. We were both just as susceptible to the pain that permeated our skin. And I can't help but wonder which is better: a "wise fear" for what the future might hold, or a childlike wonder without worry.

I'm beginning to understand that the answer to this question, like most everything in life, lies not in absolutes but in nuance. Navigating our experiences without adequate regard for safety isn't only irresponsible, it's ignorant, like walking into a busy intersection blindfolded. On the other hand, viewing life through the lens of inevitable imminent danger is like living in a haunted house. We carry a sinking sense of dread and anxiety that comes with certainty that threats loom around every corner.

As someone who once viewed the world through a fear that wasn't wise and wreaked havoc on my mental health, all I can say is that my perception became reality. Consuming excessive quantities of alarmingly negative news and books and surrounding myself with circles of folks simmering in the same sort of fear made how I experienced and interpreted everything around me, including my everyday life, more negative.

And if there's anything to the so-called laws of manifestation, it's that the seeds of what's possible are first sown in our minds. If all we see is the potential for stings when we look to the outside world, then we'll perceive the world as a very dangerous place, indeed. But if we can make a conscious move to cultivate a more positive and optimistic mindset, we not only reach a more realistic, enlightened understanding of the subtleties and dual-sided nature of all that exists, but we also see the world more clearly. An unequivocal view of the world as dangerous and dark is just as limited and incomplete as viewing it as all "love and light." The world, and its "bees," are meant to be seen for everything they are, their essence and exquisite entirety.

So, while we must be aware that bees sting, we must not sacrifice the simultaneous awareness that they're also one simple, yet critical, component of the delicate environmental design that sustains us.

Fortunately, all the stings that one stuck insect inflicted on my sweet boy haven't stopped him from returning to the outdoors and spending endless hours in the sun kicking his soccer ball. That painful experience only made him more resilient.

And unfortunately for me, I've met many more "bees" in the decades since my earliest encounter. Friends I thought would never betray me. Romances I thought would never end in heartbreak. Professional endeavors I thought would never end in embarrassment. And young love I never thought would end in death.

After so many stings, it can feel impossible to remember who we were before life pierced us the first time. It might not be realistic to believe that we can return to the pureness of perspective we possessed before we realized that some bees would wound us. Still, I can't help but think there's significance for that solitary little girl swimming in the buggy pool.

Who was she before being stung was possible? How much wider open was her heart? She was lighter when she viewed life through another lens.

With openness instead of judgment.

Optimism instead of cynicism.

Trust instead of suspicion.

Artistry instead of ugliness.

I'm not sure understanding the darker side of bees ever stopped me from getting stung, but I do know the world felt different after that. Somewhere along the line, I started interacting with the world head-first, instead of heart first—viewing it through fear instead of fondness. And now, I can't help but wonder whether this journey of life is nothing more than unpacking all the buggy baggage to uncover the beauty of "bees," again.

CHAPTER 34

Tattoos & Taboos

When we mirror others for approval, we lose sight of where they end and we begin. Familial pressure to be more palatable disconnects us from essential pieces of who we were born to be—people often more interesting, kind, fun, loving, happy, and content than the personalities we struggle to fit ourselves into.

Tattoos used to be taboo to me.

Getting one was something I'd never do. Etching ink images into my skin seemed too unconventional and unsafe for the way I saw myself. Every thought, move, and minute of my existence (with but a few alcohol-induced exceptions) was controlled and inhibited. My voice was meticulously measured, and any self-expression that might've been deemed unappealing was subdued, if not squelched altogether. When words are chosen with the same degree of care as selecting wedding china, it's impossible not to be stiff. My values might've been liberal, but I behaved conservatively.

A body with tattoos was too bold for me. I chalked most people's decisions to tattoo themselves up to the likely consequences of lapses in judgment or control, or deliberate attempts to be subversive and buck the status quo. *Why would anyone want to corrupt their flawless physical canvas?* I wondered. And when curiosity gave way to condemnation, *Those tattoos won't be so pretty at seventy,* followed by, *Besides, I'm not a biker babe.*

Smugness aside, tattoos scared the shit out of me. Their permanence made me uncomfortable. I mean, sure, one might adore an image, phrase, or person enough today to imprint them on themselves, but how could they be certain that preference wouldn't change tomorrow, or next year, or in a decade? The art on their appendages may resonate with them for a moment in time, but then in a matter of months or years, repulse them.

I couldn't conceive of committing to something so permanent because everything about my unhappy-achieving self was impermanent. All of me was dependent on external circumstances, cultural expectations, and social conditioning, so it was always subject to change. Who I was wasn't solid because I had no true north. Instead, I was as malleable as clay.

I couldn't be the kind of woman who got tattoos simply because most people I knew didn't have tattoos. And they were the ones whose approval my contrived identity hinged on. The same young woman who believed she'd never tattoo herself is the same one who thought she was just like her mother. Yet, neither of those assumptions proved correct.

Today, I'm an almost-middle-aged woman with tattoos, and I'm very different from the woman who birthed and raised me. I'm not better or worse, just distinct and divergent in many ways. The most visible of which might be that my mother has no tattoos, and probably never will.

When we mirror others for approval, we lose sight of where they end and we begin. Familial pressure to be more palatable disconnects us from essential pieces of who we were born to be—people often more interesting, kind, fun, loving, happy, and content than the personalities we struggle to fit ourselves into. Not only do our mirror selves require us to betray who we are to behave in accordance with external notions of who we're meant to become, they also render our souls closer to dead than alive. Our spirits are meant to soar, not stay at cruising altitude in perpetuity.

Tattoos themselves aren't the point. After all, no one can be defined by appearances alone, whether their skin is bare or inked with a plethora of self-dictated pictures. My tattoos are only outward signs of significant inward shifts:

From a woman who cared too much about others' opinions—to one embracing her birthright to be herself.

From a woman who strived to be perfect—to one who sees poetry in her imperfections.

From a woman whose body was used for everyone else's benefit—to one who claims it as hers alone.

From a woman who conformed to cultural definitions of beauty—to a nonconformist redefining beauty for the first time.

From a woman too ashamed to tell her stories—to one showcasing them on her skin.

My first tattoo includes the birth dates of my three children. It wraps around my left rib cage and hugs my heart. It symbolizes more than the three most meaningful souls in my life and the days they entered the world. Rather, it represents the unconditional, unadulterated love I have for them. It's an illustration of my feeling that they're the embodiments of my heart leaving my chest, even as I breathe.

Another tattoo of mine, on my right wrist, depicts a snake eating its tail in the shape of an infinity symbol. A serpent consuming itself is known as an ouroboros, an ancient representation of time as cyclical, as something that flows back into itself like a water wheel and engages in endless cycles of regeneration. Just as snakes shed their skin and start anew, the tattoo signifies my own journey of self-healing and inner renewal. It reminds me that the past is present, and the present will soon be past; and to view enlightening expeditions of the soul as life-long, if not eternal, endeavors.

The next tattoo I've planned for myself will be the number thirteen in Babylonian numerals on the side of my left forearm. In ancient times, thirteen was associated with feminine energy, and Friday the 13th was a holiday that celebrated goddesses and the divine feminine. However, it became branded with unlucky connotations by the beginning of Christianity, as the number thirteen is thought to be a reference to Judas, the thirteenth guest at the Last Supper.

One goddess encouraged me to venture into tattooed territory in the first place. My friend Julie has bright red hair, eyes that sparkle like the sun reflecting off ocean waves, and a smile so bright you can't bear not smiling back. She jokes that we are soulmates because when she met Aaron at work, she believed we were destined to become friends the minute he showed her my picture.

To say that Julie is fashionable would be a severe understatement; at least one room in her home is routinely utilized as a closet. She collects clothes and shoes like some people collect stamps or shot glasses. Her interests and tastes are fascinatingly eclectic, and her personality bubbles over with free-wheeling fun. Julie has already acquired almost a dozen tattoos and intends to get more. And she isn't a woman who works in the arts or in an explicitly creative vocation; she's a health-care executive with a PhD.

Despite her conventional workplace, Julie doesn't hide who she is. She won't cover the tattoos that tell her story or wear boxy suits that hide her body. She arrives at work every day as herself. One day she might be wearing a tunic and square-toed boots, the next she might be wearing a lace dress with a frilled collar and fishnets. Being brave enough to be herself in a setting where others typically aren't, or aren't allowed to be, isn't easy. Julie's been dress coded (always by women in senior management positions) more than once. She's had sexist rumors about her spread around the office. But despite all the bullshit that being herself brings, she refuses to show up as anyone else. She knows that who she is—is enough.

Julie isn't afraid to be feminine, whether through her clothing or her body art, if it's done pursuant to being herself. She's been dubbed "bohemian" by most of the world for most of her life. When she expresses herself, she'll sometimes qualify her preference or perspective with: "I know, I know, I'm bohemian! I've always been told that. But ... "

Bohemian is a word used to describe nonconformists. It refers to anyone who dares to be different. And by different, I mean anybody who doesn't do things in accordance with the limiting, narrow, arbitrary rules we're coerced to follow. Someone who won't sacrifice authenticity in favor of complicity.

So, I admire my beautiful, bohemian friend Julie. For her sincerity.

Her courage. Her inspiration. Her realness. Her funkiness. Her femininity. Her body art. And we'll keep tattooing ourselves—smiling together in the face of any social taboo that tells us not to.

CHAPTER 35

Godmothers

♥

*Beholding a woman who gives no fucks about being infallible is like
being in the presence of an empowered goddess. Her own admission of
herself as a mere mortal makes her a feminine force to be reckoned with
because she isn't afraid to fail. Criticism loses some of its sting when
we never profess to be anything other than imperfect.*

I didn't believe in God for most of my twenties and thirties, but I
always believed in my godmother.

As a child, I questioned why my mother asked a cousin she hardly
knew to be my godmother. She told me it was because she was baptiz-
ing me in the Catholic church, and her cousin Claire was Catholic at
the time. Apparently, Catholicism was the deciding credential for the
woman responsible for my religious education.

So, I didn't really know the woman who signed the cards and sent
the gifts I received on birthdays. I recognized her face from infrequent
family reunions and photos on holiday greeting cards, and she bore a
striking resemblance to my grandmother, her aunt. Claire was taller
than my grandma, but they shared the same lean "Harrison legs," petite
frames, button noses, and smiles. It wasn't until college that my relationship with Claire went from occasional correspondence to close.

The small liberal arts college I attended wasn't far from her suburban neighborhood, and she made it a point to treat me to lunches at
places I couldn't afford. The more I got to know Claire, the more she
became not just a godmother but a mentor.

She exposed me to a generosity I wasn't accustomed to. I witnessed her open her wallet to every stranger on the street who solicited us, giving without question or expectation. She gave because she cared, and because she could.

She came from the same family and surroundings that I did, one without much in the way of white-collared professionals or college degrees, in a place that was more rural than rich. And although she became a mother, she built a career before building a family, breaking tradition with at least two generations of women before me who birthed babies when they were barely old enough to be eligible for undergraduate diplomas. It wasn't that the choices of the other women in my family were less righteous; it was that Claire's choices reflected the path I wanted to pursue for myself.

From a business background to a degree in horticulture to a stay-at-home mother to a member of the clergy and community activist to a Lyft driver, Claire wouldn't be boxed into any one occupation. Her spirit is too big to be labeled, and her talent is too vast for limits. Although she's led an impressive life, she isn't concerned with impressing anyone. Quite the opposite, in fact. Claire doesn't care to be anything but herself, in whatever profession piques her interest at a particular point in time. She accepts and understands that she is constantly evolving.

Once, in a casual conversation about perfectionism, she remarked, "I'm not perfect, and I don't ever try to be." Her comment caught me off guard because at the time, all I'd ever tried to be was perfect. Perfect was the perpetual benchmark against which I measured myself. So naturally, self-hate ensued every time I fell short of that unattainable standard. Seeing someone so flippantly dismiss the suggestion of perfection as pointless fascinated me. It was as if in a single offhand observation, Claire handed me another key to unlock the ever-elusive, internal door to freedom from unhappy achieving.

Imposing perfectionism upon ourselves makes any sort of personal peace impossible. We're so flawed, fumbling along through unforeseen mishaps and miscalculations. To accept this universal reality, to fully acknowledge our humanness, requires us to admit that perfection is not just an illusion but a delusion. By recognizing that we'll inevitably fall short no matter how earnestly we strive for flawlessness, we are rid of the pressure to please others at the expense of truth and authenticity.

It also allows us to examine our shadows in earnest, seeing sides of ourselves that we'd otherwise push away or vow to correct whenever perfectionism tells us they're too terrible to exist. But releasing resistance in favor of wholehearted reckoning is the place where imperfections become transformed into superpowers.

Beholding a woman who gives no fucks about being infallible is like being in the presence of an empowered goddess. Her own admission of herself as a mere mortal makes her a feminine force to be reckoned with because she isn't afraid to fail. She never hesitates to reimagine herself in new roles because she doesn't worry about making mistakes. Claire embodies the belief that nobody can tell her something about herself she doesn't already know. Criticism loses some of its sting when we never profess to be anything other than imperfect.

A few weeks after *Roe v. Wade* was reversed, Claire left me this voicemail message:

Hi, Ash, it's Claire. I'm just calling with my condolences about our FUCKING COUNTRY!

[A pensive pause ensues as she realizes I might listen to her message with my three children within earshot.]

Oh, I hope this isn't on speaker phone! Anyhow, you have a kindred spirit in Savannah, Georgia! Just calling to say hey, and I love you. Take care, honey! Bye now!

My godmother's perfectly imperfect sentiments soothed my soul. Her unconditional love and unwavering presence are precious to me, and I can't help but see her benevolence as a lifelong blessing.

I may have stopped believing in God for a while. But I never lost sight of the significance of one outspoken, well-chosen, marvelously mortal godmother.

CHAPTER 36

Suffering

*Healers are those who have stepped toward their own suffering,
stared into its depths, and resurrected themselves from darkness to tell
tales of trauma and tragedy that create resilience. They teach us that
brokenness isn't a barrier to wholeness, but its beginning, a holy place
where a path to wholehearted living unfolds.*

I like to infuse my mornings with other people's advice and wisdom.
This often takes the form of reading books with daily passages
intended to inspire inner reflection and self-examination. I enjoy this
practice because, like magic, the guidance offered in my reading often
bears striking relevance to my own present struggles.

The tidbits of knowledge I glean from the authors' experiences are
like cheat sheets for my challenges. If I don't know what I'm doing,
and no one in my circle seems to know either, I can search an author's
insights to help me make sense of my circumstances. After all, no one's
experiences are the same, and no one's experiences are truly unique.
Recently, though, I noticed a disturbing theme in my morning passages: suffering.

"I'm so annoyed," I complained to Aaron one morning, while feeling
harried amid the weekday routine.

"And why's that?" he asked, without glancing up from the three
plates of breakfast food he was assembling for our hungry children. His
question, coupled with the slight quiver in his voice, signaled he was
curious and cautious about the answer he was about to receive.

"Well, suffering's a recurring theme in my daily reading lately. It almost feels like some sort of cosmic subliminal messaging that I must be suffering, too," I vented. "And I don't get it, because I'm not. I feel fine."

Aaron finished spreading peanut butter on a bagel. Then, like an oracle steering me toward understanding subtleties I couldn't quite decipher, he said, "Maybe the suffering isn't yours."

Just like that, he served me a heaping helping of uncomfortable truth for breakfast. Aaron may be intuitive, but it probably didn't take psychic powers to see that I'd spent almost two weeks avoiding some-one else's distress.

A situation I didn't know how to handle weighed heavily on my mind. Someone I used to be friends with had recently endured the dev-astating, horrific loss of her husband, who died in a car accident on his way to work, and I wasn't sure what to do. Ordinarily, I would have dropped everything and gone to her, offering to be with her and trying to help however I could. But I wasn't that person for her anymore. Although we weren't enemies, and I felt love and gratitude for what we once shared, we weren't exactly friends, either.

The last time we talked, she'd told me she thought the two of us had grown apart. We hadn't spoken in nearly nine months, and I wasn't sure whether hearing from me would even be welcome. But I knew one thing for certain: I'd rather do nothing than do anything to cause her more grief.

I knew I couldn't comprehend all she was going through, and I hoped I never would. No one should. However, I had experienced the incomprehensible pain of losing someone I loved with my whole heart in a sudden, excruciating way. I endured the wrench of having him ripped away without the opportunity to say "goodbye," "thank you," or "I love you." I knew how surreal it was to wake up to a normal day, then have your world shattered by a single phone call. And I hated hearing of anything like that happening to anyone else, let alone someone I used to be close to.

For days after I heard the news, my mind raced. I ruminated, wept for her, and prayed that the right thing to do would present itself. *Should I call? Should I go to her? Should I let her be and respect the reality that we no longer had a relationship?* These questions played on repeat in my brain until I finally decided to write her a letter.

I didn't know if she wanted me to reach out, and I was scared if I offered my heart, it might be rejected. I understood that this was an old unhappy-achieving tendency based upon the limiting belief that heartbreak is best avoided by protecting one's own heart. Now, though, I knew better: fear, anxiety, protection, and judgment block and obstruct our ability to experience the emotions we most deeply desire, but open hearts and unconditional love attract and elicit the same.

So, I did my best to let go of my insecurity and listen to my soul. And my inner knowing said that sending sincere support to someone suffering is the right thing to do, regardless of how it's received. If it's performed without expectation, in earnest, and in a manner that respects the other's well-being and boundaries, being unconditionally loving toward those in pain is our spirit's calling, if not humanity's collective mission. Our lowest selves hold grudges; our highest selves let go in love. Only fear and ego trick us into ignoring this heart-centered wisdom.

I promised myself I'd write the letter as soon as the words came to me. I believed if I was patient, they'd reveal themselves, and I'd know what to say to bridge the distance between us. So, I waited.

When Aaron called me out in the kitchen, I was still waiting. I hadn't written anything yet and had told myself the words would come in their own time. Now I realized the longer I waited, the more I allowed myself to wade knee-deep in my own bullshit. The delay wasn't related to figuring out what to say. That was a story I told myself, rather than facing the reality that I couldn't sit with my friend's suffering long enough to put pen to paper.

Telling myself I was holding off until magical words manifested in my mind was misguided. There are no enchanted verses to console someone during their darkest hours. There's only love. And when darkness almost consumes us, the most we can hope for is light surrounding us from every possible source.

Yet, we tend to forsake those who are suffering.

Their agony makes us uncomfortable, so we turn away. We do what's expected according to the social dictates that direct our lives, and then we move as far from another person's misfortune as possible. We make meals and send flowers, and then we disappear. We tell ourselves we must return to our daily routines, but the fact is, we can't stand to stomach suffering longer than we have to.

A friend of mine who was raped said that after her assault, the people she was closest to abandoned her. And it made me wonder which was worse for her—the assault itself or the isolation afterward?

I thought I'd made my peace with suffering. That it no longer made me afraid or inspired internal resistance. But I'd lied to myself. And the lack of a simple letter to help another soul in the throes of unspeakable suffering proved it. I spent almost twenty-five years avoiding my grief and despair over Dan's death. Did I honestly think reckoning with my own suffering somehow made it less unsettling to me? If so, I underestimated how terrified human beings are to suffer.

Still, despite such universal reluctance, those who've suffered greatly grow into our greatest healers. Not healers in the sense of medical professionals (although some certainly are), but individuals who've inhabited enough hurt to develop the deepest capacity for compassion and empathy. Healers are those who have stepped toward their own suffering, stared into its depths, and resurrected themselves from darkness to tell tales of trauma and tragedy that create more resilience. They remind us that suffering isn't just cursed ugliness, but rather an energy that can be transmuted into blessed beauty with time and attention. And they teach us that brokenness isn't a barrier to wholeness, but its beginning, a holy place where a path to wholehearted living unfolds.

Being a healer isn't a static status; a healer is anyone who meaningfully shows up and holds sacred space for someone else's suffering. We can't be effective healers for everyone, but authentic healers know suffering when they see it and strive to offer support.

In my case, I wasn't showing up. I was scared. But I could extend love in a letter. No one alone can heal anyone else, and no one alone can heal the world, but we can become conduits of healing for one another. And even if that level of collective healing won't change the world, it will at least make it more humane—so no one ever has to suffer in silence again.

Sometime after sending my letter, I received this text message:

Hi, Ash. I got your letter. Thank you. It really means a lot to me.

CHAPTER 37

Halves & Wholeness

The connections we feel for one another have nothing to do with the physical forms that house the sacred substance of our souls. Whatever parts of ourselves pain and suffering force us to shed over a lifetime are accounted for by unconditional love, and by the sight of our imperfect selves in the eyes of those who don't notice our broken pieces because they never lost sight of our wholeness.

On an ordinary morning, someone I love woke up and went about her day, but by the time she went to bed that night, a part of her was missing.

Doctors removed my family member's foot due to a disease she'd underestimated. Most of us don't anticipate suffering before it knocks on our door, dropping in on our lives like an uninvited guest. We don't volunteer to host it or welcome it in, and it still moves in and insists we accommodate it. It's immune to privilege and resistance. It's impolite and pisses us off. It compels us to scream and ask why the fuck it chose us and our houses to set fire to. And the only answer it ever gives is: *Why the hell not you?*

Perhaps that's why we're so culturally drawn to cinematic depictions of other people's pain. We avoid it in our own lives and the lives of those around us, but we experience a catharsis from watching this universal experience happen to strangers. Someone is suffering at the center of any dramatic film worth watching. We make movies about war, cancer, divorce, and death—anything that scares us and cuts us to the core. A movie about a perfect day would be about as interesting as a novel about salt. Suffering is hard to sit with, and we spend most of our waking hours wishing it would never find us or those we hold dear. So why does it remain solidly at the center of not just our art, but our collective consciousness?

Because it's universal.

Because it's the subject of the stories that speak to who we are, and who we're born to become.

Because it's the place where pain pours out and vulnerability rushes in.

Because it dismantles our masks, so our souls shine through.

Because it renders the impenetrable parts of us porous.

And lets oceans of love cleanse us in lifesaving waves of compassion.

My friends used to tease me that I had a sick obsession with movies in which men suffered some sort of life-altering affliction. *Dying Young*, *The Painted Veil*, and *Stronger* all made their way into my video library. For a long time, I couldn't explain what it was about a man's suffering that sang to me. Now I realize it wasn't the sight of their suffering that moved me. It was the exquisiteness of them being laid bare—and the breathtaking ways others blessed them by bearing witness to it.

Sometimes suffering, in all its excruciating, traumatic messiness, is the only thing that allows others to see us, truly see us. Behind defenses we've built. Behind the ego that obscures our essence. Behind the armor hardened around our hearts. When suffering incites the brutal storm that breaks us down—when its clouds of darkness reduce all we thought, believed, and took for granted to crumbling rubble—we see ourselves, not as unhappy achievers but human beings, for the first time.

These moments of trial are moments of truth. They are pivotal points at which we're confronted with a choice that charts the trajectory of our subsequent existence: let suffering crack us all the way open so we can choose to expand our capacity for empathy, or close off and shut out all the unexpected beauty suffering ushers in to bless us.

Suffering itself can't kill us. It's how we respond to the choices it brings that establishes the difference between life and death—between spending the rest of our years residing with those who are the most alive or as another member of the walking dead. The decision is ours alone. Suffering is our chance to save ourselves and inhabit living more fully.

We numb ourselves and avoid suffering within and around us, but we still, safely, seek it out in books and on screens because we know that stories of suffering make us feel something. We're desperate to *feel*. Emotions, even those suffering brings, remind us we're alive. They rip us out of emotional deprivation and reawaken us to the depths of our experience.

Bodies are fragile and finite. They bend and break against our will. They grow old and frail, like cruel cages for the eternal aspects of us enhanced by the years that line our faces. The connections we feel for one another have nothing to do with the physical forms that house the sacred substance of our spirit. Whatever parts of ourselves pain and suffering force us to shed over a lifetime are accounted for by unconditional love, and by the sight of our imperfect selves in the eyes of those who don't notice our broken pieces because they never lost sight of our wholeness.

To them, we are more than what the world recognizes. More than our parts, more than the physical and emotional wounds that slice us in half. We're complete because we are beloved. And they remind us that regardless of what may befall our fickle bodies, our essence isn't easily shattered. Suffering is, after all, a window of opportunity to transcend the mundane, matter-of-fact, material existence of yesterday in favor of the meaningful, soul-centered life of tomorrow.

And that doesn't require two working feet—just one willing heart.

CHAPTER 38

Homework & Healing

We are the books yet to be written. Our souls are the epics we see in our dreams. We can make every aspect of our existence more beautiful, again and again. Growth isn't easy or uncomplicated; yet it inevitably increases our capacity for gratitude, joy, and love.

The healing required to unbecome all the bullshit we mistook for ourselves takes more than a session, a season, or a several-month span. Being alive is a lifetime commitment to cultivating our spirit.

A friend, exasperated by her ongoing struggle to find more inner peace, recently said to me, "I've tried everything: therapy, yoga, Reiki, acupuncture. You name it, I've tried it. I've read all the self-help books, and nothing seems to work in the long run."

I felt for her. Finding a way through our own suffering and struggles can seem like walking through quicksand. All we want is someone or something to share the secret to standing strong on solid ground. Still, I worried the answer my friend sought might be one she wasn't necessarily ready to hear.

Because there is no secret. There is no mystical modality that lessens the hard work of healing. Any resource that resonates with us is merely a tool, not a cure. It's an external means to point us in the direction of doing our internal homework. No matter how enlightening or impactful the mechanism may be, we're the ones who must show up day in and day out to shovel our shit.

For me, that's taken many forms. Sometimes, it's called for more time in meditation; at others, it's journaling to process through pain. At its worst, it meant more minutes crying in the shower than I can count, allowing the water to serve as a channel for releasing feelings I can't otherwise let go of. It can also be a conversation with a friend who is like family and will hold a space for my hurting heart, or taking time for myself in nature.

Whatever shape shit-shoveling takes, it's courageous work. It's the ultimate hero's journey, abandoning the safety and familiarity of a life left behind to brave the uncertain, embattled terrain of self-healing. Nothing is more terrifying than exploring our inner landscape with the same energy and commitment once solely reserved for our outer world because we feared what we'd find.

Before the universe set me off on an unanticipated internal expedition, I genuinely believed nothing bad had ever happened to me. I used to tell people that I'd never experienced any true trials or trauma. Others had baggage, but not me. My life was too perfect and privileged to possess pain meaningful enough to imprint itself upon me.

This mindset is about as believable as someone who insists they just walked three miles through city streets barefoot without getting dirty feet. It's not just improbable; it's fucking impossible. If we're breathing air and being here, we're going to be harmed in ways that destroy our defenses, burn through our brains like battery acid, and scar us. No one escapes unscathed. But before we unearth the broken bits of us we buried, it's easy to deceive ourselves into thinking we're somehow the only human on the planet who's just been hangin' out—dodging, bobbing, and weaving to avoid a whole world of hurt.

So, anytime I hear someone express similar sentiments, my heart swells with love and compassion for the parts and pieces of them their past suffering prevents them from seeing. I hold inner space for the preciousness of their invisible, yet palpable, pain. I know there are significant aspects of themselves they can't access because they locked them away long ago when someone said they were unsafe or unsavory. And I send out a silent, sincere wish that when they're ready and willing, life will lead them to unlock the doors to healing.

Once we endeavor to open even one door, we find that every door leads to another. Healing is a continual corridor through life. To truly live means that growth, change, and elevation are endless. This means that the mere notion that any healing modality will ever "heal" is misleading. The goal isn't to attain a healed state. Such a state might not even be human. However, you can aim to increase your inner fulfillment and feel more fully alive. The intention behind self-healing isn't perfection, but to perpetually polish facets on the diamonds of our soul selves so we shine brighter.

Healing is a conduit to a higher state of existence. And shifting attention away from the external to the internal is the first seedling of self-love. But only we have the natural resources necessary to farm our lives and reap the harvests of our hearts. The time, attention, and dedication required to till the soil of our past can be possessed by none but ourselves. No healing modality can replace the patience, perseverance, and hard work of a farmer tending to her land. And if we don't labor upon it, what could have blossomed with abundant beauty becomes barren.

We can make every aspect of our lives more beautiful, again and again. Growth isn't easy or uncomplicated; yet it inevitably increases our capacity for gratitude, joy, and love. After all, life involves intentional evolution. Sacred flow. Continuous change in motion. Stagnation, on the other hand, is a slow, unintentional, emotional death. We must consciously embrace the struggle and befriend the pain necessary to uncover the infinite potential buried inside of us.

We are the books yet to be written. Our souls are the epics we see in our dreams.

It's up to us to pick up our pencils, our lucky pens, or our laptops, and create new, richer, more authentic narratives for ourselves. We can unhook from the trap of unhappy achieving to embark on our own unbecoming. We are the healing agents waiting for us to be ready to unburden ourselves, so we can be lighter. Healing is homework in a class that doesn't end until we're dead and buried. If we spend our time searching for quick fixes and shortcuts, we may not exactly fail the course—but we certainly cheat ourselves.

CHAPTER 39

Valuables

\ ι /

Most things I've acquired meet their eventual end in a dumpster or donation center, regardless of how desperately I wanted them once upon a time. When I declutter and detach myself from previously held perspectives about what's worthwhile, I identify all the artifacts of my existence that actually make my life worth living.

The things that mean the most to me are worth the least to the rest of the world.

I'm a minimalist. At home with my three children, I combat clutter like a farmer trying to protect her harvest from locusts during a biblical plague. The attempt is futile but necessary if I want to preserve my preferred way of living. Never mind that my household probably places enough annual Amazon orders to pay all of Jeff Bezos's utility bills; and my children are dedicated collectors of stuffed animals, fad toys, and cheaply made tchotchkes. I still try.

To keep the items in our house from overtaking it, I engage in periodic clean-out days. These unfortunate events are typically spontaneous, announced by me to my family without forewarning whenever the general disarray or junk accumulation in a particular corner of our living space so offends my minimalistic sensibilities that I can't stand it a minute longer. It may sound severe, but it's either pare down some piles of shit or watch the woman of the house lose her shit as she envisions herself drowning in a sea of shame created by consumerism.

Sometimes, though, I don't bother eliciting the help of my family in my single-minded, slightly obsessive mission to rid our collective quarters of excess. I take matters into my own hands via quiet, covert decluttering operations.

In other words, I donate my family's belongings behind their backs.

This is dangerous business for obvious reasons and has backfired on me more than once. For instance, Crock-Pot cooking (as well as cooking of any kind) wasn't among my proficiencies when I got married, so I gave the Crock-Pot gifted to me for my wedding to Goodwill. Then, when my grandmother introduced me to a Crock-Pot cookbook I liked, I had to buy a new one.

Wasting money repurchasing items I once owned isn't the only pitfall of my commitment to keeping mess to a minimum. The most upsetting outcome of my arguable obsession occurs when one of my children occasionally utters the question that stops me in my tracks: "Mom, where's my [insert any material good marketed to children on YouTube here]?" Because it would conflict with my very Buddhist commitment to honesty, I don't lie. So my ensuing answer sounds something like: "Oh, honey, I'm sorry. I donated it because I didn't think you played with it anymore."

The response that comes next dictates my subsequent move. If my child shrugs their shoulders and doesn't seem too bothered, I release the tension in my abdomen from holding my breath and exhale in relief. Problem solved. But if, alternatively, my child reacts in a manner that signals distress, I launch into profuse apologizing, brandishing my phone in their direction and promising that the Internet gods will deliver them a new one ASAP.

Ninety percent of the time, my children don't notice the things that disappear like magic from their toy bins or dresser drawers when they aren't looking. But when they do, I harbor a secret fear that one of my babies will grow up to be a bona fide hoarder, complaining to an expensive therapist their insurance doesn't cover that their mother caused them permanent psychological damage by throwing away prized possessions.

There are, of course, the untouchables: those timeworn, tattered, cuddled-to-death objects of my children's affection that none of us would dare tamper with, let alone discard. My son Ari's "blankie and puppy," my daughter Alexandra's "foxie" and accompanying fox throw, and my son Ashton's "lamby." If any of the above go missing, minutes feel like months until they're back in my sweet babies' adoring arms again, though the sight of these ravaged, stained rags would make most strangers cringe. Despite needing an overdue bath or all-expense paid trip through our washing machine's heavy-duty cycle, we treat them with a reverence once reserved for saints and royalty.

For all the neuroticism that compels me to fight clutter with the conviction of Marie Kondo, sentimentality also keeps me hanging on to collections of keepsakes. My children's keepsake boxes contain exceptional artwork, birthday cards, and tender mementos. Mine consists primarily of past pictures and presents they gave me, special cards and notes, and anything that feels meaningful or suggests something special about my journey. When my kids sort through my memorabilia after I'm dead and buried, I hope they learn things that make them say, "Oh my God, I never knew this about Mom!"

My box of memories is probably only a fraction of what many people hang on to for nostalgia's sake. Still, there are two things I've always kept close: the ring Dan gave me when we were seven years old, and the picture of him his mother sent me. It was the last photo she took of him, snapped on his first day of seventh grade, just a few days before he died. In it, he has the brooding expression of a boy becoming a teenager. However, the softness in the corners of his dark brown eyes and slight smile signal a son appeasing his mom by posing for yet another first-day-of-school portrait.

His picture is glued to a blue backing with the words "A friend is a gift you give yourself" scrawled underneath it. I tore it out of a scrapbook a family member made for me when I was a kid because I wanted to keep it next to the ring Dan gave me. For most of my adulthood, I stored the ring and picture together in a nightstand next to my bed. One night, though, I dreamed that a stranger in my house stole the ring from my dresser, so I relocated it to a spot that seemed safer as soon as I woke up.

Any thief would be disappointed to discover that the ring isn't worth anything. I imagine Dan thought it was real when he stole it from his grandma. But fortunately for everyone involved, it was costume jewelry. I doubt either of our mothers would have let me keep it if its "diamond" center was anything other than fake. The ring is a gold flower with ebony petals unfolding around a cubic zirconia. It's so old that the actual ring beneath the flower setting detached many years ago, and all I have left is the bud it used to hold. I once took it to a jeweler to see if they could reattach a gold band beneath it, but they said it was too fragile. Its old age and poor craftsmanship make it impossible to wear, refresh, or repurpose. It has no financial value. And yet, except for my wedding ring, it's the most personally valuable possession I have.

What does it say about us in an unhappy-achieving country consumed with stockpiling success in the form of money and material wealth when all the things that move us most over a lifetime fit in the palms of our hands? Or, when what wakes us up at night isn't the fear of losing a fancy car or a flat-screen TV, but the terror of someone stealing the remaining remnants of a ring left behind by a long-dead, but beloved soul?

Most things I've acquired meet their eventual end in a dumpster or donation center, regardless of how desperately I wanted them once upon a time. But I see through the stuff that distracts me from what matters when I set aside the toxic lessons I've been taught about what's valuable and where my values should lie. When I declutter and detach myself from previously held perspectives about what's worthwhile, I identify all the artifacts of my existence that actually make my life worth living. Grasping what's precious; letting go of the crushing analyses and judgments that dictate my other choices; and assigning true value, time, and attention to simple, yet significant things.

Sometimes, those belongings aren't the ones society says to strive for. Because often what the world deems least significant—we hold most dear.

CHAPTER 40

Rules

True, unconditional love cannot be tamed. It cannot be confined.
It cannot be stomped out by someone else's self-righteousness. It cannot
be mitigated by the arbitrary, yet mandatory, brand of morality our
culture requires us to adopt.

I used to believe rules kept me safe. Now I see that so many of society's rules were merely indispensable parts of the unhappy-achiever programming that kept me caged. What I mistook for moral laws were actually cultural masks for man-made measures intended to tame wild hearts and women.

I used to believe that love in our hearts is real estate reserved only for our husbands and wives.

That our capacity for love is so narrow and finite that it can't exist outside of the context of a committed partnership or romantic relationship.

That love requires possession or ownership.

That love includes expectations and obligations.

That our lives and our loves can belong to anyone but us.

These are a small sampling of society's bullshit rules about love. Rules that bastardize a sentiment that, in its purest form, knows no conditions, no rules, no qualifications. Because the truth is this: *true* love seeks nothing except someone else's unadulterated happiness.

True, unconditional love cannot be tamed. It cannot be confined. It cannot be stomped out by someone else's self-righteousness. It cannot be mitigated by the arbitrary, yet mandatory, brand of morality our culture requires us to adopt. It burns independently of whether we feed it or stoke its fires. It breathes even after we cut off its oxygen. It beats steadily in its chambers, even when our awareness detaches from it.

Love doesn't know the world's rules, and even if it did, it wouldn't care. It persists despite disparagement and deep denial. It sits quietly in the inner sanctum of our consciousness, content to wait there whether it's ever recognized or reckoned with. We can curse it and condemn it. We can curse and condemn ourselves for feeling it. Nevertheless, it abides in our being, unabashed and unfazed.

We can lie to ourselves and others, disavowing a sacred source of light so no one accuses us of darkness. It doesn't blame us for this dishonesty. It understands that the world knows nothing of it. If it did, the world wouldn't work so hard to restrain and contain it. It wouldn't be so uncomfortable with its presence anytime it doesn't meet narrow, patriarchal prescriptions and expectations. And it wouldn't become so resentful of those who don't measure it out to themselves like medication or baking flour—those who allow themselves all the love, even when it breaks the world's bogus rules.

About six months after I was consumed by the grief I'd stowed away in the aftermath of Dan's death, a person I confided in about my experience sent me an email. She wrote that if her spouse acknowledged a soul connection with someone else—as I had acknowledged about Dan—she would be "hiring a lawyer." The message she sent sliced through my stomach, striking as swift and sharp as any rhetorical bullet shot at me ever had.

In her mind, according to her rules, the penalty for a love that became part of me years before puberty was divorce. Her worldview dictated that my husband should divorce me for admitting that aspect of myself. Because only his love was allowed to inhabit my heart. Because my heart should remain the exclusive domain of the man who married me. Because I didn't deserve to hold on to all the love that life offered me along my journey—I could only accept the love represented by the wedding ring on my finger.

These ideas, these judgments, these rules, tortured me. Guilt and shame racked my brain as I longed to lean into a love that returned to me after grief opened me up to it again. A list of self-chastising statements rang through my consciousness like scratched records of other people's resentments: *Your feelings are bad. Indulgent. Silly. Senseless. Illicit. Illegitimate. And immoral.*

But if what I feel is forbidden, I thought, *why does it feel so goddamn good? And why did it resurrect itself after I buried it?*

I went on like this for a while, trying to withstand and win an internal wrestling match between what my heart wanted and what my head—and the world around me—said. Then, finally, a friend shook me out of my silent misery.

"Ash, whose rules are these that compel you to rein in your own heart?" she asked me. "Are they the rules of pastors and priests? Are they the rules a patriarchal order imposes on the female sex to subjugate it? True, unconditional love is never intended to punish—but to bless. It's only our own limiting beliefs about it that torture us. So why, my darling, are you following any rules other than your own?"

She was right. I was being disloyal to myself to pacify other people. Abandoning an aspect of me so inextricable from my identity that the only way to exist without it was to accept a partial life. Sacrificing a piece of me since I was seven years old in service of somebody else's fucked-up sensibilities. And for what? For other people's fickle approval? For external acceptance and validation according to an arbitrary code of conduct? For the sake of friendships with a few folks who weren't really friends, anyway?

That night, on a couch, with a glass of wine and cool candlelight burning in the background, in the presence of a person who respected me enough to encourage me to break the rules breaking me down, I erased the restrictions that used to run me, and started writing—and living—according to directives I defined for myself.

Not long after that, I was at an Alanis Morissette concert with Jenni, my friend since elementary school. Jenni was the girl who held my hand through many of the hardest moments of my childhood. She's the one whose impromptu hug propped me up as I collapsed after seeing Dan's dead body. She has also accompanied me on more free-wheeling adventures and wily escapades than I can count, so I was excited for us to go to the concert together.

We arrived on time, but as we waited for the concert to start, the clouds above the amphitheater turned black. Lightning flashed, and thunder bellowed, drowning out the opening act's drumbeats. It never ceases to surprise me how, despite spending decades with someone, there are still things about them that startle us. I found out that day that Jenni is terrified of storms, as I watched her wrap herself in a trash bag as if it were a bulletproof shield. While I was amused by the irony of the opening act playing "Only Happy When It Rains" during a downpour from the heavens, my friend grimaced and pulled her homemade poncho tighter.

I could see her eyes widen with every audible crack across the sky. Meanwhile, the rain drenched the uncovered bleacher seats, making them impossible to use. Neither of us would see Alanis if we didn't figure out an alternative seating solution fast. I encouraged Jenni to put her garbage-inspired ensemble back in the wastebasket and swore to keep her safe, and her panic gave way to the perseverance I remembered from adolescence.

"See that man?" she said, gesturing toward an amphitheater employee checking tickets for the covered sections of stadium seating.

"Yeah," I said.

"As soon as he turns his back, we're sneaking behind him and snagging those open seats," she said, nodding toward six vacant chairs several aisles down.

I hesitated. "Jenni, are you serious? We're going to get caught!"

"No, we're not," she said. "Trust me, Ash. We got this."

"We're bucking some serious rules here, sister," I said. It was my last attempt to convey that I was less than eager to join in the crime I was about to commit.

Jenni flashed me a sinister smirk and said, "Rules are made to be broken, baby." Then she slithered behind the unsuspecting stranger whose sole job was to ensure we stayed in rain-saturated seats. Despite my doubts, and my disingenuous desire to be a compliant concertgoer, a little co-conspiratorial mischief orchestrated by my friend resulted in not only dry seats but also a night of dancing and singing together to some of the most beloved songs of our youth.

While I can't condone stealing concert seats, I can say that reevaluating and rewriting the rules around me has been revolutionary. It's been an indispensable act of reclaiming my precious existence as my own. The only way to ensure we're living fully liberated lives is to take a long, hard look at the rules we once mistook for moral truths, especially when they trap our hearts and trivialize our happiness. If we're not living on our terms, life becomes less of the blessing it is intended to be and more of a terminal sentence. Rules can render us more dead than alive, depriving us of our innate right to love beyond what most people perceive as possible.

Incidentally, no one ever showed up to claim the seats Jenni and I stole, and it seemed to us that those spots had been magically saved for us: for two women willing to take a chance—to trade being girls who were good for being women who were a little bit bad.

CHAPTER 41

Free Spirits

As I inch closer to becoming a middle-aged woman, I live as loud as my aunt Pat's laugh, let my soul soar, and lead with an open heart.

I was born with my spirit free, my heart open. Then, sometime before I became a woman, my heart closed, and my spirit began its confinement.

My aunt Pat is a free spirit. Even a Catholic convent couldn't cage her. Her bellowing laugh bounces off the walls of whole rooms, and she smiles so fully that the rims of her eyelids curl upward like happy half-moons. My father's adoring older sister, she never had children of her own. Instead, she filled the space motherhood would have occupied with her nieces and nephews. Time spent with Aunt Pat as a kid meant weekend lessons in lightheartedness and fun-loving spontaneity.

I could never predict what we'd do or where we'd go as we set out on our carefree adventures. One visit might include rated-R horror films forbidden by my parents, while the next would involve a surprise trip to a Western wear store to buy cowboy boots to support my short-lived interest in country line dancing. I boot-scootin' boogied better than before in the white-leather, fringed boots Pat got me, or at least it seemed like I did.

Recently, I hosted my aunt, now nearly seventy years old, at an annual party for friends and family Aaron and I threw at our new home. As I showed her around our property, she paused more than once to offer a warm hug, brimming with the familiar, earnest energy I remembered from my childhood, and whispered: "God bless you, sweetheart. God bless you."

Afterward, we walked together for a while longer and caught up on the years that had passed since we last saw each other. I felt moved to mention how much I'd changed, so I muttered matter-of-factly: "I'm a free spirit now, Aunt Pat. I didn't know it for most of my life, but I know it—and live it, now."

My unprovoked proclamation made my aunt waver. She cast an astonished sideways glance at me before turning squarely to face me.

"Ashley," she said, grabbing my shoulders and sounding concerned, "you've always been a free spirit. Don't you remember?"

Then she regaled me with forgotten stories of wild escapades from my childhood, including one when we each took turns gesturing to strangers to roll down their car windows so we could inquire, "Do you happen to have any Grey Poupon?"

As I recalled each exploit, it struck me that my free-spirited aunt had spotted the free spirit in me before I'd spotted it in myself. My personal revelation was no revelation to her whatsoever. It was a truth about her niece she knew all along.

It's hard to know when I stopped being free and started being "good." It's possible that time spent with Aunt Pat was a temporary reprieve from being "good," and a safe space to be free. Maybe her presence provided precious opportunities to stop performing and relax into myself for a moment. Maybe I sensed an open acceptance in her that allowed me to express a part of my adolescent self I otherwise felt pressured to suppress.

She doesn't know how much hard work and heartache it's taken to reject my good-girl image and reclaim the joy of just being me. She doesn't understand how much being good made me feel like I could barely breathe. How I suffocated under the weight of the inauthentic life that good built. How it felt less like a fairy tale than a trap. She didn't witness how much heat I took when I chose my happiness over other people's hefty expectations. She never saw the trails of tears that streamed down my red, raw cheeks as years of suppressed pain flowed from my brain and body.

I demanded freedom.

There was nothing covert or inconspicuous about my journey of unbecoming. I grasped the bars of the cage of a "good" existence with both hands, shook them with clenched fists until my fingers bled, scrounged up every ounce of my strength, and screamed: "No more! I can't do this any longer! I want my fucking life back! I want to live and love—fully and freely—before I die!"

So I examined every voice that narrated the audiobook of my life, muted every one of them, and started listening to *me*. I looked at every person I had turned my power over to, and I took it back. I looked inward and saw walls I'd erected that kept hurt inside and happiness at bay, and I broke them down with healing.

I said no when I would have said yes.

I let go of a need for approval and approved of myself.

I traded obligation for authenticity.

I opted out of an overflowing and overfilled social calendar and surrounded myself with sisters who saw me.

I refused to accept other people's pain, projections, and judgments, and practiced the art of self-acceptance.

I surrendered the false sense of stability a good image gave me and stepped forward into an unshakable sense of self.

And slowly, steadily, I transformed from a good girl into an empowered woman.

Later that night, at the party, Aunt Pat and I danced to my father's four-piece rock 'n' roll band until long after dark. The more I jumped and moved my body to the music with mystical abandon, the more Aunt Pat's face lit up with a mixture of awe and affection that said, "That's my girl!"

As I inch closer to becoming a middle-aged woman, I live as loud as Aunt Pat's laugh, let my soul soar, and lead with an open heart. So, the rest of the world might see what my aunt always saw in me.

A kindred free spirit.

CHAPTER 42

P!nk Idols

*Sometimes we put people on pedestals, believing that if we could
be just like them, our lives would be happier. But the only difference
between them and us is that they refuse to subdue the parts of
themselves the world wants to punish them for. Instead, they burn
bright and true. And humanity, in all its darkness, can't stop itself
from beholding the glow from their stars.*

I used to idolize other women and hoped I could be like them.
Gloria Steinem was my deity growing up. She embodied the divinity of my adolescence, and I was her doting disciple. It was odd for a kid from rural Illinois, raised in the '90s, to become enthralled with a feminist revolutionary fifty years her senior. Second-wave feminists certainly weren't part of my parochial elementary school's curriculum. If anything, they would have been seen as Satan's abortionist spawn, rather than history-makers. But I saw something in Gloria that helped me make sense of myself.

My conservative school and community, set in the rural farmlands of northern Illinois, always felt both foreign and like home at the same time. I belonged there in the way we belong to the places we're born and brought up in, but I struggled to shake the feeling that I wasn't meant to be there at all. I was different, and the main difference my brain could discern was that I appeared to have a much bigger problem with injustice than anyone else.

Being treated differently, especially based on my sex, was an affront my young mind couldn't abide. I knew being a woman was a blessing, not a curse. My femininity was empowering, not disempowering. And my capacity to create life was a sacred gift worthy of respect and reverence, not some sick, punitive source of political control and disenfranchisement. So, anytime I perceived that differential treatment was doled out simply because I was a girl, I reacted as if someone had set off a fire alarm in my psyche. And whenever my indignity was aflame, outraged words flew out of my mouth with abandon.

In eighth grade, a boy in my class made the blatant assertion that girls shouldn't be allowed to play football. My face got hot as our teacher asked him why he felt that way. "Well, I mean, how's a girl supposed to tackle a two-hundred-pound lineman?" he asked, seeming satisfied with himself.

My hand shot up.

"Yes, Ashley?" our teacher said, unable to ignore the abrupt wave of my arm.

"Well," I said, staring directly at the boy whose statement infuriated me, "the day any dude in this class actually has the ability to take down a two-hundred-pound lineman, we can talk about how girls can't play football. Until then, girls should be able to play."

My teacher smiled, and the discussion ended. I didn't want to debate which sex was stronger, but I couldn't let bullshit—blanket rules, intended to deny everyone a fair chance to play—stand.

That's what Gloria Steinem meant to me. She represented someone unafraid to fight for fairness, to take a stand for other people's freedom to play. She wanted us to be unencumbered and unrestricted by arbitrary rules that do us a disservice and make no sense.

Gloria's example gave me permission to be myself in a hometown that seemed like it would rather not have me. She inspired me to create ways to disrupt in a religiously conservative school, where disruption wasn't only discouraged, but strictly condemned. She personified possibilities beyond the limiting beliefs and lies I was brought up with about girls, boys, and everyone in between. She was an iconic reminder that it didn't matter if you came from Toledo, Ohio; or Marengo, Illinois, there was enough space for all of us, even if folks in the city I was from didn't think so.

If my childhood infatuation with Gloria resulted from her impressive historical record of patriarchal resistance, my passion for P!nk was due to nothing less than that she seemed to epitomize sheer feminine rebellion.

When P!nk's single "Don't Let Me Get Me" came out in the early 2000s, I was captivated. *Who the hell is this woman with bubblegum-colored hair?* I wondered. She was a stark contrast to every other young female singer in mainstream music. In my late teens and early twenties, the ideal image for the so-called fairer sex promoted across media platforms was basically bleach blond, big breasted, small waisted, and not particularly smart. I fit almost none of those criteria. It was radical to see someone my age brave enough to take on Tinseltown by being herself and singing about the same programmed self-hate that led me to puke in parking lots.

I love rebel women.

I love women who are a little bit (and a whole lotta bit) rock 'n' roll.

I love women who are bold enough to be real.

I love women who rock boats, especially ones who don't ordinarily get rocked.

I love women who are righteous without being self-righteous.

I love women who are unafraid to roar about their pleasure and their pain.

And so, naturally, I fucking love P!nk.

Although I dreamed of meeting both my idols, I'm not sure I ever seriously thought I had a shot at being introduced to either one. Then, last winter, an invitation to "An Evening with Gloria Steinem" magically manifested in my Twitter inbox. I didn't know how or why my desire to meet Gloria was fulfilled without warning, but I wasn't going to question it.

A couple of months later, I sat four feet away from Gloria Steinem as she answered questions and shared revelations acquired after over half a century of revolution. (When another attendee asked whether the

Supreme Court would reverse *Roe v. Wade*, she said she was optimistic they wouldn't. Sadly, she was wrong.)

The longer I listened to the woman I spent a lifetime wishing I could be, the more I realized she wasn't so different from me, after all. She patiently responded to every audience inquiry. The rest of us hung on her every utterance like the next word would be a Christlike epiphany regarding the way forward for those of us worried about women's rights. Although her responses were eloquent and informed, I couldn't ignore the fact that she clearly didn't have the answers we wished for any more than we did.

In that moment, I realized I was the woman I always longed to be. The reason I was drawn to Gloria Steinem and P!nk, the reason their lives, experiences, and songs spoke to me, was because they embodied aspects of myself. I am a writer and speaker like Gloria. I am an artist and rebellious truth-teller like P!nk. The women I idolize most—I am—and they are me.

Sometimes we put people on pedestals, believing that if we could be just like them, our lives would be happier. But the only difference between them and us is that they refuse to subdue the parts of themselves the world wants to punish them for. Instead, they burn bright and true. And humanity, in all its darkness, can't stop itself from beholding the glow from their stars.

At the event I attended with Gloria, I handed her a note of gratitude, letting her know how much she inspired a lonely little girl who needed a hero to hang on to. An email landed in my inbox a few months later from the office of Gloria Steinem, requesting my mailing address because "Ms. Steinem read my letter and wrote a reply."

Her words are now framed above my writing desk in the handwriting of someone who meant so much to me:

Dear Ashley,

Your letter itself is such a big reward! Yours are the kind of words that make this work worthwhile.

I thank you for putting hope in an envelope.

With friendship, Gloria

CHAPTER 43

Rights & Wrongs

It's taken me until almost midlife to see the rights in this litany of wrongs. To make sense of suffering imposed upon my soul and remove myself as the victim in my life's stories. To fully integrate the liberating belief that I no longer have to internalize external wrongs.

"What's wrong with me?"

This is the question I asked family and friends whenever something in the world suggested I was inadequate, strange, or insufficient. "Ashley, there's nothing wrong with you," they'd say, exasperated. But I couldn't accept that. "Please tell me, please! I can take it," I'd plead, with desperation and despair.

They'd offer me no answer to satiate the insecurity inside me. This self-doubt was the product of low self-esteem, cultivated and pruned to perfection by external callousness and cruelty I mistook for fair feedback. It took me a long time to learn that although other people's nonsense was directed toward me, most of it wasn't about me.

I wish someone had let me know that simple fact when I was young. Instead, early on, people told me I was *too shy*. And yes, I was shy. Sometimes my mother would take me to a playdate or birthday party, and by the time I was ready to join in the fun, it would be time to leave. I internalized being quiet, contemplative, and cautious as being socially inept, deficient, and inferior.

What I learned: *I am not outgoing or extroverted enough to behave as I am expected to in public.*

The same girl who was too shy was also told she was too chubby. When I became too old for round cheeks to be considered adorable, meals went from sources of comfort and satisfaction to punishment and humiliation. A relative who sometimes babysat me liked to chastise me at the dinner table. Before I could bring a utensil to my mouth, "Slow down, Ashley. This isn't a race. You don't need to eat so fast," rang out across the table, stomping out my appetite with a surge of shame. The implication was clear: if I didn't slow down and stop eating so much, my young body wouldn't be accepted.

What I learned: *I take up too much space. I need to be small to be accepted and liked.*

My body wasn't my only physical trait that family members and peers taught me to despise. A nose I inherited from my grandfather became a genetic curse, rather than a paternal blessing. "She looks like a member of the Goof Troop," said a boy I went to high school with, suggesting my nose resembled that of a Disney cartoon-character dog.

"You've got your grandpa's Jewish nose," family members laughed, unconcerned by the racial stereotyping.

"You're so beautiful, Ashley. But my God, that nose!" someone blurted out at a holiday gathering in front of my high school boyfriend. The message was clear: I would be beautiful, but for the unfortunate center of my face. Long before I became an adult, I came to believe that becoming aesthetically pleasing was contingent on cutting off a part of me. So, at nineteen years old, I cobbled together all the money I'd saved in my life and paid every cent to a plastic surgeon, in hopes that he could carve some of my pain away.

What I learned: *I was born with a nose that didn't meet racist notions of feminine beauty.*

On my first day as a legal clerk in a court of law, I wore the bland, navy-blue, pinstripe skirt suit and black pumps I'd bought for internship interviews. Law professors advised me that this was the exact attire professionals in my field would expect to see a young woman attorney like me wearing. I hated skirt suits. I felt most empowered in a black pants suit with a basic button-up, collared shirt and comfortable dress shoes, and felt disempowered by the conservative feminine uniform I wore instead.

I don't know if it was the outfit, the list of legal skills and accolades on my résumé, or both, but I landed a part-time position at the district attorney's office near my law school. As I waited for court to begin, standing before the bench with a stack of case files, I worried about whether I'd know what I was doing when the judge emerged from his chambers.

A middle-aged male attorney with slicked-back hair strutted toward me. He smirked as he moved close enough to breathe on me, stroked the fabric of my suit jacket on my shoulder, and said suggestively, "Hmmm . . . this is nice. What's it made of?"

Stunned, the most I could muster was: "I'm not sure." I was twenty-four years old, yet suddenly, I felt fourteen, and with that, another man had diminished me.

What I learned: *I was a woman participating in a profession that remains a masculine domain.*

The first time I was betrayed by a female friend, I was in eighth grade. My friend was angry that I had performed better than she had at basketball, which she felt was her sport. Instead of sharing the spotlight with me, so we could excel side by side, she started a rumor that I was romantically involved with a basketball coach. I found out about the painful lie at a basketball camp we attended together when a fellow camper confessed: "She said you have sex with a teacher."

Ridiculous! Absurd! I hadn't had sex with anyone *ever*, let alone an adult!

The next day, a tearful confrontation ensued, culminating in the last words she ever spoke to me. With her face as solemn as I'd ever seen, she made it clear that she was unmoved by my overflowing emotion. At the very least, I wanted an apology, but I wasn't going to get it.

"My mom says I don't have to talk to you," she said.

What I learned: *I invite backlash when I outshine the person who pretends to be my friend, and I earn the penalty for jealousy in female friendships—betrayal.*

Recently, Aaron and I were strolling down a city street on our way to a wine bar for our coveted date night. As we stood at a crosswalk, waiting for cars to pass so we could continue on our way, the warmth of the sunlight on my face was almost as blissful as his admiring glances. I was wearing a new dress and had taken extra time on my hair and makeup, all of which made me feel radiant. Taking the time to dress up was a luxury for a mother of three, working from home in the summer, so I soaked up the opportunity to feel glamorous and enjoy Aaron's adoring gaze.

Our reverie was soon interrupted when a man in a pickup truck pulled up alongside us and called out to me.

"Hey, hey, girl!" he yelled so loudly that he startled me, making me jump.

"Who's he talking to?" I asked Aaron.

"Well, he's staring at you," Aaron said. The tone of his voice signaled shock and disgust at the audacity of a fellow man.

I glanced over my shoulder to catch a glimpse of the guy catcalling me as his vehicle rounded the corner. He was still staring at me, and shouting gibberish I couldn't make out. I took a breath, collected myself, and we went on our way. Aaron was also shaken, though. He had witnessed what it's like for a woman he loves to walk a city sidewalk on a Saturday night.

This experience was familiar, one I'd encountered in every stage of life since puberty. But when it happened as my husband held my hand, it achieved another level of indecency and personal indignation. As a woman, it was an occurrence I was at risk of whenever I was by myself, but now it had occurred in the presence of my partner. And for some reason, that made the humiliation of it hit me harder.

What I learned: *A woman appearing in public is an open invitation for disrespect from men.*

It's taken me until almost midlife to see the rights in this litany of wrongs. To make sense of suffering imposed upon me and remove myself as the victim in my life's stories. To fully integrate the liberating belief that I no longer have to internalize external wrongs. To transcend outer pain with inner strength. So, I leave the wrongs that present obstructions to my path in my wake and walk ahead with both feet. I step over them now, instead of stumbling on them.

And I transmute them from a lifetime of grievances that once chipped away at my spirit into this bill of rights I abide by today, from the wrong to the right:

The wrong: *I am not outgoing or extroverted enough to behave as I am expected to in public.*

The right: *I behave in accordance with who I am, not who others wish I was.*

The wrong: *I take up too much space. I need to be small to be accepted and liked.*

The right: *I fill myself to the brim with all that nourishes me, body and soul, starving for nothing and no one.*

The wrong: *I was born with a nose that didn't meet racist notions of feminine beauty.*

The right: *I define femininity and beauty for myself, free of the notions, standards, and narrowness of a sexist system.*

The wrong: *I was a woman participating in a profession that remains a masculine domain.*

The right: *I call out sexism in every setting, until the day masculine domains don't just tolerate women, but revere them.*

The wrong: *I invite backlash when I outshine the person who pretends to be my friend, and I earn the penalty for jealousy in female friendships—betrayal.*

The right: *I show up and shine my light, attracting and allowing only those with shared values of love, loyalty, and abundance in my circles.*

The wrong: *A woman appearing in public is an open invitation for disrespect from men.*

The right: *I affirm my birthright to be in public spaces and be respected—while looking and feeling however I please.*

Making these kinds of proclamations can be powerful for all of us. I invite you to define for yourself the terms of your life—the rights and wrongs that are right for YOU. Embodying these laws empowers us to right past wrongs and heal pain perpetrated upon us by other people. Although I'm flawed and fundamentally human, there's nothing wrong with me. There's nothing wrong with you. And there never was.

CHAPTER 44

Prayers & Peace

This is the purpose of a prayer. It is an opportunity to reconnect with, rediscover, and reopen to the beings we were when we were born. Prayer allows us to recall versions of us who once acted without ulterior motives and weren't motivated by ego or malice, who sought to bless the world and be blessed by it, in earnest.

When I was a child, my knowing was innate. The more I grew, the more my mind connected with outer truths, the more I lost touch with myself.

I prayed every night as a kid. For a long time, I believed that the habit became compulsory because of my parochial school indoctrination—that it was something I did simply because teachers told me to. Recently, though, I realized it was more than that. Praying was a practice that provided solace, a safe haven for my young spirit to turn to for help and healing. Emotions, especially difficult ones, weren't dealt with in my family, so quiet moments in my bedroom became sacred opportunities to pour all of me into a solitary spiritual cup.

Prayer took me to a place I knew and didn't know all at once.

A place beyond my conscious awareness but palpably present in my psyche.

A place my body couldn't touch but my being seemed sourced from.

A place not proven but evidenced by my soul.

There was something therapeutic about speaking my deepest hopes and hurts aloud, and I repeated the same incantation every night:

Dear God,
Please keep me safe and healthy, protect me and guide me.
Please keep my friends and family and everyone else safe and
healthy, protect them and guide them.
Please help me achieve all my goals and dreams.
Please forgive me for all the sins I've committed.
And please bless every living thing, especially my friends, family,
and everyone else.
Amen.

The recitation above remained relatively unchanged throughout college and law school, except for a litany of specific goals and dreams that varied over time. They shifted with evolving interests and pursuits. Nevertheless, I carried this prayer, crafted in early elementary school, with me until I met Aaron. I don't know what compelled me to keep it. I had rejected all the religion I was raised with years before I ever stopped chanting this sincere song in the stillness of evening silence.

The last time I spoke it, I shared it with Aaron. We were lying in bed, exchanging stories about our religious upbringings, and I decided to disclose my nighttime ritual. As I pronounced every word of the secret spell I'd cast for myself for decades, it sounded starry-eyed and silly. Aaron didn't say much afterward, and I interpreted his lack of response as an indication he thought so, too. Shame set in almost immediately. In that moment of embarrassment, I abandoned the daily devotion that kept my heart company for so long.

I sacrificed something that day, and it was more than the security and reliability of voicing my most intimate dreams and desires regularly. Pressing my palm against the invisible glass confines of everything that cages in our humanity, and whispering, "I'm here, and these are the wishes I want to manifest for myself and the world." That was a piece of it, of course, but it was more than that. My childhood self, the one who folded her hands in faithful prayer, understood something my adult self didn't see: Every prayer is a chance to hold holy space in our hearts for ourselves and others.

And whether the prayer is secular or religious, spontaneous or scheduled, isn't important. It doesn't even need to be named "prayer," if the connotations of that term make you uncomfortable. Call it meditation, contemplation, self-reflection, or manifestation. Label this personal practice whatever you like—as long as it's performed from that point of purity we all possess, even if we struggle to access it the longer we're alive.

It's the pureness so apparent in infants and young children that we marvel in the midst of its Divine presence. The fact that it falls away from us as we mature leads us to believe it's nothing but naivete. However, its familiar comfort makes us wonder whether it's possible to resurrect the purity we abandoned in ourselves, and whether that purity might relate to the "something more" so many unhappy achievers seek when all else seems senseless.

This is the purpose of a prayer. It is an opportunity to reconnect with, rediscover, and reopen to the beings we were when we were born. Prayer allows us to recall versions of us who once acted without ulterior motives and weren't motivated by ego or malice, who sought to bless the world and be blessed by it, in earnest.

It's understandable to feel weighed down, worrying about what the world needs to end its suffering and questioning what any one of us alone can do to make a dent in the mass destruction and devastation around us. But what if individual acts of meditation could manifest multitudes of external acts of goodwill? What if private prayers could heal the people who will heal humanity? What if bringing about a more benevolent world requires masses of people who first focus on finding their own intrinsic benevolence again?

Don't pray because you're pressured to. Don't pray because you're afraid not to. Don't pray because a pastor or priest told you that the penalty for lacking piety is eternal punishment in hell.

You can pray because you've lived in the absence of faith in anything and everything.

You can pray because your heart is so heavy it's aching to unburden itself.

You can pray because the part of your soul you've lost touch with is calling out to you.

You can pray because you're sick of suffering.

You can pray because a chaotic culture of disconnection and discrimination is bringing you down.

You can pray because a world riddled with war needs you to save yourself so you can save it.

You can pray to privately cultivate your own peace.

You can pray for the world to be a more compassionate place for all of us.

You can pray because you are part of the world—and you are worth praying for, too.

CHAPTER 45

Scotland

nu-

*At a time when my life looked more uncertain than ever, I prayed
that putting my bare feet on green Scottish moss might bring me
back to myself when I needed me most.*

I wasn't sure if boarding a plane to Scotland less than a month after I
ended my marriage was lifesaving or self-serving.

Perhaps it was both. I had no idea I'd be separating from my husband of fifteen years when I signed up for a two-week tour of the Scottish sacred sites, but that's what happened.

As my plane touched down in Glasgow and the lush green landscape left me in awe, an email headed "Goodbye, Ashley" landed in my inbox. Aaron said it was his way of letting me go gracefully, though it felt more like a kick in the gut than a kickoff to my trip. I was optimistic about the adventures the Highlands held for me, but the message from my husband reminded me of the mess back at home.

Traveling to Scotland by myself felt fitting. For years, I have had a recurring dream where I am in the midst of a Scottish forest. The trees are so tall they look as though they brush up against the bottoms of the clouds. Their dense thicket creates an emerald roof overhead, and only a thin sliver of sunlight sneaks through the cracks. It isn't much, but it's enough to illuminate my face. My chin is upturned toward the sky, desperate to absorb every bit of energy emanating from the breathtaking wonder surrounding me. I'm alone; and all I feel is the soft, smooth velvet of green moss underneath my bare feet. The dream is so vivid and clear that it feels like a glimpse of me in another life, and now, having just left my husband, I sensed this was another life, after all.

When I left for Scotland, I wasn't speaking to most of my extended family. I'd always joked that if Aaron and I ever divorced, they'd disown me and adopt him. Suddenly, their reactions to my desire to dissolve my marriage made that statement more of a premonition than a joke.

My family attributed all the differences they observed in me in recent years to "a phase," a temporary foggy headedness that would one day clear. They couldn't see the changes inside of me that coincided with the outside of me:

I had become an activist of love, an artist, a seeker of the collective good.

I had let go of those who preferred me to be inauthentic, and I had found soul sisters who loved my sincere self.

I was no longer a dutiful daughter, desperate for my family's favor.

I was no longer a woman who could stay safely in the confines of an unfulfilling marriage, and instead had made the dangerous decision to ask for a divorce.

Nothing about this was easy. I couldn't cite a single socially acceptable reason for divorcing my husband. He was faithful and devoted. He was handsome and supportive. He was my best friend. Yet something was missing.

We weren't connected in the ways we should have been, and we hadn't been for a while. Intimacy—emotional, physical, and spiritual— was a struggle.

I wished the problems between us could be resolved through couple's therapy, but I knew the distance between us couldn't be bridged by counseling, and I couldn't justify putting Aaron—or myself—through months of meaningless motions that wouldn't alter our eventual end. Divorce was our destiny. And although it was dark and disturbed every plan we had ever made for ourselves and our family of five, we couldn't ignore its call.

Women may have come a long way, baby, but "good" women still aren't supposed to end their marriages to seek higher levels of love and satisfaction. Historically, women who dared such things saw themselves beaten into submission or spending the rest of their lives in sanatoriums and asylums.

Fortunately, contemporary social sanctions for women like me are more subtle. One friend's husband simply told her he didn't want her associating with me anymore, as if divorce was a disease she could catch.

You're selfish, Ashley, they probably wanted to say to me. *Shame on you for fucking up your family for your own sake. Spread your legs once a week, smile, and shut up about it.*

I walked away from a life most would envy. Aaron had been recently promoted to his dream job, and we had just moved into our forever home. Aaron was the primary breadwinner, while I had no money, no plan, and no idea what the next days, months, or years would look like.

Standing in truth might be righteous, but its repercussions can be ruthless. The first time I stepped foot on Scottish soil, I was suffering from insomnia and borderline malnourishment. I'd always prided myself on my ability to sleep soundly, but since I'd realized my marriage was over, I'd spent every night chasing rest and every day attempting to sustain myself. When several days came and went without a hunger pang or restorative night, I knew I needed a serious course correction. I couldn't continue the way I was, and I couldn't turn back.

Just make it to Scotland, I told myself. *Scotland will save you.*

At a time when my life looked more uncertain than ever, I prayed that putting my bare feet on green Scottish moss might bring me back to myself when I needed me most. Being away from my children was brutal. I'd never been without them for so long before. Still, I understood that something significant—even if it was still intangible—awaited me in Scotland.

If there's a remedy for a broken heart, it's being surrounded by the most emotionally intelligent people you've ever met. I embarked on my travels with two seasoned tour guides and sixteen strangers who saw my grief and responded with wisdom and encouragement. We traversed the countryside for twelve days via ferries, planes, and hours-long van rides. Anytime thoughts of what I'd left behind weighed heavily on me, I'd find myself wrapped in a warm embrace without speaking a word. Such unsolicited hugs were welcome. They eased the incessant ache reverberating throughout my body from being out of harmony with those I hold most dear.

My mother loves me as best she can, and she's a dedicated matriarch. But the fear and anxiety she embodies is the same fear and anxiety her mother embodied, and the same fear and anxiety she taught me to embody. I wasn't in touch with my mother for this very reason—I couldn't muster the courage to divorce my husband in the face of my mother's fear. As a result, I felt motherless. I don't know if other women on the tour intuitively sensed this, or if they were moved to mother me because I was the youngest in our group. Either way, they nurtured and mentored me in countless ways I craved.

Cameron, one of our tour guides, was especially wise and calm. She was soft-spoken, yet her presence was commanding in a way that signaled she was a woman in her power. She and her hysterical, history-loving husband, Glenn, guided us on our journey, sharing secrets of the land and asking us to reflect on how the earth spoke to us.

Early in the trip, I began to see that Scotland wasn't going to save me by sending me something, but by relieving me of what no longer served me. The Highlands helped me release emotional wounds I couldn't carry forward into the new, truer future I was forging for myself, extracting pain so ingrained I could scarcely perceive its perpetual pull.

A series of healing conversations and interactions from sympathetic souls on my tour culminated near a cairn in the Kilmartin Glen. As I approached the monument, I reflected on all the moving moments of emotional support and release that occurred throughout my trip. I was granted immeasurable gifts by new friends I barely knew, as if they'd been brought forth to fortify my embattled being before I returned to the fight on my home front.

"When you head home tomorrow, remember you're not alone," Cameron told me. "I've stood where you are, leaving a marriage for a new life. You're strong, Ashley. You can do this. And you have the community you've found here to help you along the way."

Tears streamed down my face as she kissed my cheek. It's difficult to deny being part of an invisible plan when people you don't know you need give you exactly what you need when you need it. Cameron and every member of our Scottish Highlands crew somehow managed to move my steepest inner mountains and make room for small miracles to manifest inside me.

Still blurry eyed from my brief conversation with Cameron, I meandered over to an opening in the ground almost completely covered by stones. It was just large enough for an average-size adult to crawl into. Having seen another person slither in and out of the inconspicuous spot a few seconds ago, I thought, *What the hell?* and crawled inside. I hardly had time to settle into my claustrophobic space when my friend Lynette's face appeared in the crevice separating my dark surroundings from daylight.

"Would it be okay if I got in there with you?" she asked.

"Sure," I said.

Lynette is a light, and not just in the way people who radiate positivity and passion are. Her brilliant crown of beaming red curls bounces up and down against her shoulders in a way that's majestic. She is the embodiment of fire.

Permission granted, Lynette seated herself behind me. Suddenly, the recognition that we weren't separate women, but ancient feminine archetypes, swept through my state of mind. She was the mother, I was the maiden, and the slice of Mother Earth we sat in was a womb, holding us both in Her natural embrace and gestating what was about to be born.

"Lean against me," Lynette said.

I relaxed against her chest. She wrapped her arms around me and began breathing waves of energy through me. I felt a life force permeating every cell of my being, an infusion and an extraction. She suffused my psyche with words summoning me to let go of the shame, guilt, and suffering she sensed in me. Past traumas formed their scabs with each blessed breath.

"You don't have to carry your mother's and grandmother's pain anymore. It's not yours, Ashley," she said. "Let go of your guilt over leaving your marriage, too. Let it go."

I was stunned. I hadn't told her anything about my maternal line, nor had I shared how racked with guilt I was over the divorce. She just knew.

I wept. I wept in a way I never had before, as stagnant emotional weight poured out of me to be soaked up by Scottish earth. I cried, and I healed.

I can't say how long the healing took. But afterward, I felt hazy, as if my consciousness extended three feet beyond my head. My body tingled, and I could hardly catch my balance. Our friend Lee Anne steadied me until I could stand alone. I was almost nonverbal. My mind couldn't make out what my body and spirit just experienced.

Somewhere in the bowels of Scotland, I'd been cleansed.

Nothing died. But what was already dead, heavy, and hurting deep inside me disintegrated. There in the Glen, with nothing but space, sisterhood, and a bit of breath work, Lynette unburdened me.

The woman who reminded me of blazing fire had burned all that was broken and festering inside of me. And I arose from the smoldering ashes of my past to reckon with the unknown road ahead—free, clear, and brand-new.

Truth-Telling
for Happy Achievers

*I won't shy away from bearing witness to the most beautiful parts
of my journey because I'm afraid of other people's ugliness—I won't
allow their misplaced pain to tarnish my truth.*

My creative expression used to be like brushing my hair with a fine-tooth comb. I'd untangle the slightest hint of a knot that might make someone uncomfortable.

Writing this book was an exercise in ridding myself of the kind of self-imposed censorship that was once second nature. The words on its pages are my truth, and they aren't always pretty or pain-free for me or the people in my life. Nothing is shared with the intention to slight, criticize, or offend. Even experiences that reflect what I once internalized as external "wrongs," those that offended my sensibilities or broke my heart, aren't expressed with an aim of retribution or motivated by malice.

On the contrary, I forgive any so-called sins against me or inflicted upon me that are articulated in these anecdotes. Their power over me evaporated the moment I fully inhabited my power; and I felt their accompanying sting, grief, and sadness fade away. Forgiveness is much easier to find once we embrace the feelings that expand our capacity for empathy and compassion, looking upon them like familiar friends rather than mortal enemies.

Suffering is as universal as ecstasy and joy. We can't help but grant those around us leniency for their mistakes and missteps, hoping they might do the same for us when we similarly stumble. In this way, we understand that what we once perceived as sins or fatal flaws were neither; they were simply the unpleasant aftermath of imperfect people learning (and teaching) significant lessons.

The lessons that inspire us to change our lives—to abandon old ways of living, challenge the beliefs that hold us back, and break the cycle of compulsive behavior that prevents us from living mindfully—are often painful. Although this is merely a compilation of the facts and circumstances that created this recovering unhappy achiever, as well as the experiences that led me back home to myself, there may still be those who don't like, understand, or find resonance in what I have to say. Some may even hate it or hurl insults. And that's okay—because this isn't for them.

This book is for my former self, first and foremost, and for every unhappy achiever like her. It chronicles the becoming that began after birth, and the process of unbecoming that began when I finally allowed grief to light my heart on fire and set my spirit free. I share my stories with unconditional love.

The sort of love musicians sing about and movies portray.

The love that ends wars and inspires sonnets.

The love we imagine in our most hopeful dreams and pray for when the worst strikes without warning.

The love that forces us to stand up against fear and step forward into faith.

The love that lets us know we're alive.

This love is precious. It's pure. And it's potent enough to make us believe it must be eternal.

Some may feel skeptical when I tell them about this kind of love. And that's okay, because I don't abide by the speculations, judgments, and limiting beliefs of others anymore.

We can each live our truth and speak it without qualification or apology. We don't need validation or approval. We don't have to worry about who might misconstrue the meanings of our stories to conjure distorted or disturbing narratives. We don't have to take it personally if others bastardize our lives or our love to substantiate their hostility. To paraphrase a Buddhist teaching: If a "gift" of anger or resentment is offered but not received, to whom does the gift belong?

We have nothing to defend or prove. Freedom comes from making peace with the past, so the future can flow forward. These pages—their stories, songs, and prayers—are public testimonies of hard-fought healing and integrated inner peace.

Who we are is holy. Everything that happens to us—the highs, the lows, and the harms—are holy. And we don't need a priest, a pastor, a social media post, a self-righteous peer, or a professional pursuit to prove our holiness. The life-changing, life-affirming, life-giving love we seek is in us. It is us. It always was. All we must do is unbecome a lifetime of unhealthy, unhappy-achieving programming and indoctrination to uncover it.

Today, I am a happy achiever.

I am not enlightened.

I am not perfect.

But I am here.

I am inhabiting life fully, fearlessly, and on my own terms.

I am learning lessons and living out loud.

I am brave, beautiful, and messy.

I am enough, and I always have been.

Some days I sparkle, and other days I'm dull, but I always carry divinity.

I open my heart, surrendering to all the fantastic and fucked-up feelings that flow through it.

I tell my stories without requesting permission.

I try to own my mistakes and make amends.

I am tolerant, but I no longer tolerate less than I deserve.

I write my own rules and break bullshit ones.

I abide only by dictates I define for myself.

My value is unrelated to material wealth.

I believe in abundance, the sacredness of spirit, and the power of deep connections.

I forgive myself, and I am forgiving of others.

I cherish my family, but I won't martyr myself for them.

I value my friendships, but I won't betray myself to maintain them.

I honor my experiences—the bright and breathtaking, the tainted and toxic—because they brought me to this moment.

I resign myself to the consequences of existing as my full, unfiltered self.

The result is a richer, more joyful life.

You can be a happy achiever, too.

And you are love, and you are loved.

Your being cannot be distilled to a label.

You aren't meant to be domesticated.

You are too vast to be defined by narrow-minded rules and expectations.

You are too wild to be caged.

You are too courageous to let fear limit you.

You are too deserving to settle for less.

You are too worthy to worry about approval.

You are too precious to sacrifice yourself for other people.

Your birthright is boundless joy.

Your time has come to build a life that lights you up.

And finally, for once and for all, I am—you are—we are—entitled to be forever *free*.

Acknowledgments

♥

These are some of the people who not only contributed to the creation of this beautiful book but also supported me on my journey through these stories:

Adrian Morgan: Thank you for ensuring that this book's visual beauty matches its literary beauty and for "getting" this book well enough to create a design that embodies the energy of its stories.

Carrie Schaal: Thank you for being the beautiful, badass big sister I never had who makes me believe it's possible to make anything manifest.

Christopher McBrien: Thank you for being the man whose magic made this journey happen, and for being a faithful friend as I found myself along the way.

Eva Avery: Thank you for your creativity, thoughtfulness, dedication, and belief in me and this book. The moment I met you, it was clear there was no better publication home for this project.

Fay Sanders and Brigitte Salver: Thank you for your love, wisdom, unwavering support, and unconditional acceptance of me as an activist of the heart.

Jennifer Henze: Thank you for being a lifelong friend, always helping me find the "funny," and being brave (and bad) enough to break rules with me in the best ways.

Jennifer Jensen: Thank you for being a marketing mastermind, and for helping me to ensure that this book reaches all the unhappy achievers who need it most.

Julie Lavoie: Thank you for knowing we were soul sisters, and for standing by me before my journey of "unbecoming"—and after.

Kerri Balliet: Thank you for being an abiding friend and sister, and for seeing me through the stormy sea of my grief with a compassion that let me know I wasn't alone.

Kristina Valenti: Thank you for being my "twin" and loving all of me unconditionally. Also, thank you for making me and my life more sacred and showing me the true meaning of sisterhood.

Laura Mazer: Thank you for your impeccable editorial feedback and profound professional partnership, both of which helped me make this manuscript sing.

Linda Wolfersheim: Thank you for being a dear friend and incomparable "roomie" who understands that burying a beloved leaves us with grief that never dies.

Liz Catalano: Thank you for being this manuscript's editorial "eagle eye," who patiently perfected my imperfect grammar, alleviated my alliteration, and corrected some pretty—but problematic—metaphors.

Lynnette Ruppert: Thank you for scooping me up in Scotland, loving me, and supporting me with a goddess energy that soothes and inspires my spirit.

Mara Berkland: Thank you for being a lifelong mentor and friend, and for making the time to read this book when it was in its infancy.

Mom and Dad: Thank you for my precious human life. And thank you for your love, hard work, and sacrifice on my behalf. I am—and will always be—grateful. I love you.

My Sister Taylor and My ("Modern") Family: Thank you for your steadfast love and support of me, Aaron, and our children, especially as it enabled me to create this book and live (and learn from) these stories.

Olivia Bartz: Your work and collaboration were the cake topper to this manuscript—the editorial polish and finishing touch I didn't know it needed—until I did.

Stuart Horwitz: Thank you for your kindness and generosity; as well as for the expert editorial feedback that helped me make sense of these stories and gave this book chronological substance, shape, and structure.

The Wonderwell Press Team: Thank you to Maggie, J, and the entire Wonderwell team for making it possible for this book to be born. Without your hard work and commitment to excellence, the dream I held in my heart wouldn't be a reality.

My "Journeys with Soul" Family: Each of you touched my heart and saved my weary spirit during our time together in Scotland. You gave me the strength and support to keep going when I felt anxious, exhausted, and abandoned. I'll always be grateful for the unconditional love of two special tour guides and sixteen strangers.

To All My Unsung Healers: Too many people contributed to my healing and helped me come home to myself to name, but I am eternally grateful to every individual whose time and talents took me from unhappy achieving to wholehearted happiness. And I promise to live the rest of my life like a living prayer of gratitude in honor of those who have loved, supported, and stood beside me on this journey.

About the Author

Ashley Jordan, J.D., is an author, speaker, and former attorney. She has written for *The New York Times, The Washington Post, The Guardian, HuffPost, Woman's Day, Teen Vogue,* and more. She lives in Milwaukee with her three children.

AshJordan.com
unhappyachiever.com
Instagram: @msashjordan
Twitter: @msashjordan